Starting with Geese

Katie Thear

Broa

Starting with Geese

First published: 2003. Reprinted: 2005.

Copyright © 2003 and 2005. Katie Thear

Published by Broad Leys Publishing Ltd

Printed by Design & Print Ltd

A catalogue record for this book is available from the British Library.

ISBN: 0 906137 32 2

Cover photographs: Katie Thear

For details of other publications please see page 96

Broad Leys Publishing Ltd
1 Tenterfields,
Newport, Saffron Walden,
Essex CB11 3UW.
Tel/Fax: 01799 541065
E-mail: kdthear@btinternet.com
Website: www.blpbooks.co.uk

Contents

A group of the author's geese. (Brian Hale)

Preface and acknowledgments

One of my first memories is the friendly honking of geese in my home village in North Wales. The large white birds were active and voluble, grazing on the short-growing grasses of the clifftops as well as the inland pastures of the farm. No movement escaped them, but I don't ever remember being afraid of them. Our Christmas bird was always a goose. I was 21 years of age before I tasted a turkey!

Needless to say, I'm fond of geese, and have enjoyed writing this book. I hope it will prove useful to those who are thinking of keeping these stately birds, as well as to those who may already have them, but who enjoy reading about the experiences of other goose keepers.

I am most grateful to Mike Griffiths of the *British Waterfowl Association* and to Jenny Pritchard of *The Goose Club* for their invaluable help. Thanks are also due to David Scrivener for the use of photographs from the John Tarren photographic archive. There have been many other individuals and organisations who have helped in the production of this book. They are listed in the reference section.

Katie Thear, Newport, 2003.

Introduction

Whoso' eats goose on Michaelmas day,
Shall never lack money his debts to pay.
(Traditional saying).

Embden goose.
(Ludlow, 1895)

Goose is grass, it has been said, a reference to the fact that good pasture is the mainstay of the goose's diet. The domestic goose is also a hardy, outdoor bird of the northern hemisphere that does not respond well to unnecessary confinement. It is no coincidence that the goose is unique amongst farm poultry in not having been ear-marked for intensive, factory farming. It is farmed commercially, of course, but even the largest producers rear geese on grass because they know that anything else would be out of the question.

There are many who keep geese for interest, or for exhibition purposes. Some have a few to act as 'guard-dogs' to deter prowlers. As long as there is enough grass, they do well in gardens, fields or orchards. Those with extensive lakes may have visits from migratory wild geese. There are also those who are interested in ornamental geese. As some of these are from the southern hemisphere, they are less hardy and may require protected aviary conditions, particularly in winter.

Quality of care is vital! Domestic and ornamental geese need to be looked after during holidays, so arrangements will need to be made for their care in the event of any absence. Although domestic geese are hardy creatures and are not bothered by rain, they do dislike high winds. They need adequate shelter, and must also be protected against predators such as foxes.

Five freedoms are specified in DEFRA's welfare codes for livestock. They apply to all animals and birds, regardless of scale. If they are followed, the result will be contented geese.

• Freedom from thirst, hunger and malnutrition by ready access to fresh water and a diet to maintain full health and vigour.

• Freedom from discomfort by providing an appropriate environment including shelter and a comfortable resting area.

• Freedom from pain, injury, infestation or disease by prevention or by rapid diagnosis and treatment.

• Freedom to display normal patterns of behaviour.

• Freedom from fear and distress.

Geese in history

The geese of Meidum. This is the oldest painting in the world and dates back to the 4th Dynasty. (Egyptian Museum, Cairo).

The Greylag goose, *Anser anser*, is the main ancestor of today's utility breeds.

The Swan goose, *Anser cygnoides*, is thought to be the ancestor of the Chinese and African breeds.

Geese are featured in many traditional rhymes and stories, as shown by this drawing of Mother Goose. (Charles Robinson, 1894)

The Goose Club Committee (Illustrated London News, 1881)

About the Goose

They can be kept to advantage only where there are green commons.
(Cottage Economy, William Cobbett, 1821)

Geese have probably been kept by man longer than any other bird. There is evidence that they were domesticated in ancient Egypt 4,500 years ago, because their eggs were being artificially incubated there, a sure sign that a degree of selection for breeding was taking place. Wild geese had been caught by the Egyptians long before this, however, for prehistoric river dwellers trapped and netted them in the Nile delta as long as 10,000 years ago. The Greylag, *Anser anser,* and the Egyptian or Nile goose *Alpochen aegyptiacus,* as well as wild white geese, are still to be seen in Egypt today. Geese were kept and artificially incubated in ancient China, Mesopotamia (now Iraq) and Greece. To the Greeks they symbolised fertility. In Britain, the bones of Greylag geese have been found at the sites of several prehistoric settlements, indicating that they were trapped, and may even have been kept domestically, although there is no evidence to substantiate this.

When Rome was beseiged in 365BC, the sacred geese in the Temple of Juno gave out a loud alarm during the night. This alerted the Romans to the attempt at infiltration, thus destroying the invaders' element of surprise. The goose's prowess as a 'watchdog' is still put to good use today.

In the 4th Century BC, Julius Caesar wrote that the Britons did not eat geese, regarding them as sacred, but later Roman influence, after the decline of the Druids, would undoubtedly have changed the situation for the Celts. Early Welsh writings, based on older oral traditions, refer to great feasts, such as that of Caswallon, where geese were consumed in great numbers. In AD43, the Emperor Claudius referred to domestic flocks of large grey geese in Gaul. Both Julius Caesar and Claudius also mention flocks of white geese in what is now Germany. In AD30, Pliny reported that some of these, with their feet covered for protection, were herded across the Alps in order to improve the white geese of Rome.

During the first century AD, Columella describes Roman penning arrangements for geese in his work *De Re Rustica*, while Varro also wrote about them in *Rerum Rusticarum,* emphasising the advantages of domesticated geese over wild ones: *'Choose those that are big and white, as in most cases the goslings resemble the parents. Wild geese, with variegated plumage, do not willingly associate with the first, and do not become so tame.'*

Over the centuries, geese have been popular with the peasantry of Europe. In Britain, they were kept on common land, although much of this was appropriated by unscrupulous landowners during the 18th-19th century Enclosures, a factor that caused a considerable decline in their numbers as farm birds. My own family's small pastures were stolen in this way in 1814. A traditional saying was: *'Two geese and a gander will pay the rent.'* It is not difficult to appreciate the hardship that must have followed in the wake of the Enclosures all over Britain, as well as in the draining of the Fens.

In the past, it was often the task of the 'goose girl or boy' to look after the geese and drive them to pasture, and often to local markets. At Michaelmas, the feast of St. Michael was celebrated. This was originally held in October but subsequently changed to September 29th. A roast goose was the traditional meal on this occasion, a custom still followed by some of the colleges at Oxford and Cambridge. It is interesting to note that the City of London Regulations of 1383 went in for market price control, declaring that: *'The best goose shall be sold for sixpence.'*

In Britain, geese and other poultry were driven from August onwards to the city fairs and poultry markets. The droves were often very large with thousands of birds at a time. Those heading for London Cheapside, to the street still called Poultry, were particularly large. They came from Essex, Norfolk and Suffolk. Some were even imported from Holland and driven to capital. The Nottingham Goose Fair, at its peak, handled twenty thousand birds over twenty one days. This fair is still held today, although there is now little evidence of geese.

The geese grazed on the grass verges as they travelled and were also able to glean from stubble fields as they moved along. By October the roads were deteriorating, with deep ruts making it difficult for geese to manage. Stone strewn roads were also bad for their feet, so methods were devised to 'shoe' the geese for their journey, an ancient custom that the Romans had also used, as referred to earlier. Their feet were coated with soft tar and finished with a sand and sawdust mixture to provide protection during their long walk. The shoe could be peeled off upon arrival. There were also other methods of shoeing geese with felt and leather pads.

The spread of the railways during the nineteenth century gradually replaced the drovers across the country, but an interesting development was the formation of local goose clubs. These were the equivalent of our modern-day Christmas hamper schemes, in that for a small regular payment, you saved up for and were given a Christmas goose. The drawing on page 6 illustrates the practice.

An aspect of geese that played a crucial role in European history was the use of their feathers. Quill pens were used by the Romans and subsequent cultures. *'A goose quill is more dangerous than a lion's claw'*, according to a traditional saying, indicating the power of the written word. Where strong arm tactics were required, goose feather flights made arrows fly straight and true, an aspect of archery referred to by Grose in his *Provincial Glossary* of 1787: *'England were but a fling, save for the crooked stick and the grey goose wing'.* The down feathers of geese and ducks also provided luxurious feather beds - at least for the wealthy who could afford them.

Classification

If we 'place' geese in the system of classification originally devised by Linnaeus in the 18th century, and subsequently adapted over the years, their relation to the rest of the bird kingdom is as follows:

Class: *Aves* (Birds)

Order: *Anseriformes* (Water birds)

Family: *Anatidae* (Geese, swans and all ducks)

Sub-family: *Anseranatinae*
Tribe: *Anseranatini*
Species: Magpie goose, *Anseranas semipalmata*

Sub-family: Anatinae
Tribe: *Tadornini* (Sheldgeese)
Species: Egyptian goose, *Alopochen aegyptiacus*
Cereopsis or Cape Barren goose, *Cereopsis novaehollandiae*
Andean goose, *Chloephaga melanoptera*
Ruddy-Headed goose, *Chloephaga rubidiceps*
Ashy-Headed goose, *Chloephaga poliocephala*
Orinoco goose, *Neochen jubata*
Abyssinian Blue-Winged goose, *Cyanochen cyanopterus*
Kelp goose, *Chloephaga hybrida hybrida*
Magellan or Upland goose, *Chloephaga picta*

Tribe: *Cairinini* (Perching geese)
Species: Spur-Winged goose, *Plectopterus gambiensis*

Sub-family: *Anserinae* (Geese, swans and whistling ducks)
Tribe: *Anserini* (True geese)

Race:

Anser (Grey-brown geese)	***Branta*** (Black and white geese)
Species: Greylag, *Anser anser*	Barnacle, *Branta leucopsis*
Sub-species:	Red-Breasted, *Branta ruficollis*
Western Greylag, *Anser anser anser* ⎤ (Most	Canada, *Branta canadensis*
Eastern Greylag, *Anser anser rubirostris* ⎦ domestic breeds)	Ne-Ne (Hawaiian), *Branta sandvicensis*
Bean goose, *Anser fabalis*	
White-Fronted, *Anser albifrons*	Brent goose, *Branta bernicla*
Lesser White-Fronted, *Anser erythropus*	
Pink-Footed, *Anser brachyrhynchus*	
Snow goose, *Anser caerulescens*	
Bar-Headed goose, *Anser indicus*	
Emperor goose, *Anser canagicus*	
Swan goose, *Anser cygnoides* (Chinese and African breeds)	

From this table, we can distinguish between the *true geese* of the northern hemisphere and the *sheldgeese* of the southern hemisphere. Sheldgeese lie somewhere between true geese and ducks. They have the same upright stance and grazing habit of true geese but have two moults a year, like ducks. There are also southern birds that do not fit into these categories and are therefore given a separate classification. Examples are the Magpie goose of Australia which has incomplete webbing on the feet, and nests in trees, and the Spur-Winged goose of Africa which is also a climber. Some birds are called geese but are not geese at all! Examples are the African Pygmy goose and the Maned goose which are both ducks and therefore not included in the table.

The true geese are all members of the *Anserini* tribe and are hardy birds of the northern hemisphere. There are two racial groups - the *Anser* which are greybrown geese such as the Greylag and Bean geese, and the *Branta* which are black and white birds, such as the Canada and Barnacle geese.

Development of domestic breeds

As far as domestic breeds of geese are concerned, the wild Greylag, *Anser anser,* is their main ancestor. There are two sub-species however, referred to as the Western Greylag, *Anser anser anser,* and the Eastern Greylag, *Anser anser rubirostris.* The former has an orange bill while that of the latter is pink. It is no coincidence that most of the domestic breeds which evolved in Western Europe had orange bills while those in Eastern Europe and Russia tended to have pink bills. In Eastern Europe, there is a long tradition of keeping geese, not only for table and down feather production, but also for the sport of goose fighting, although this was officially banned in Russia at the beginning of the last century.

The wild Greylag has relatively static populations within its range of distribution, so it is not difficult to see that it provided a ready genetic pool that encouraged early domestication. It also has a tendency to produce random mutations or 'sports' that are pure white. These appear to have been particularly popular and were then selected, not only for their colour but also for their size and weight.

Until comparatively recently (in historical terms) there appear to have been white, grey or pied (part-coloured) domestic geese. Gervasse Markham refers to this choice in his book *The English Husbandman*, published in 1615: *'Now for the choyse of geese, the largest is the best, and the colour would be white or grey, all of one pair, for pyde are not so profitable.'*

Over the years, different areas have produced their own strains of geese, giving them names that reflect the place of origin. There was an English White and an English Grey, for example, while Germany had a German White. Russia produced the Grey Tula and the White Arsamas, named after the places as well as the feather colouring. The famous Toulouse goose of France was based on the grey geese of that area, although much larger versions, with more of a dewlap under the chin, were subsequently bred in Britain.

The outstretched neck pointing forwards is the typical warning stance meaning *'Keep your distance!'* It is adopted by both sexes. (Katie Thear)

The introduction of the Chinese and African geese into Europe enabled new crosses to take place. The Chinese and African are thought to have been derived from the wild Swan goose, *Anser cygnoides*. The Chinese produces more eggs than most other goose breeds, an aspect that would have been popular with breeders. The Steinbacher goose of eastern Germany, for example, was produced by crossing the Chinese with local breeds of the area.

In the 19th century, as general interest in poultry keeping and breeding grew, there was also a parallel interest in exhibiting birds. Breed clubs were formed and standards drawn up that illustrated the ideal characteristics of particular breeds. In Britain, the *Poultry Club of Great Britain* now represents the interests of all poultry breeds, including ducks and geese, while the *British Waterfowl Association* represents the specific interests of ducks and geese. The latest standards for goose breeds have been drawn up by the BWA, and are illustrated in the book *British Waterfowl Standards*. Breed clubs are affiliated to the main organisations.

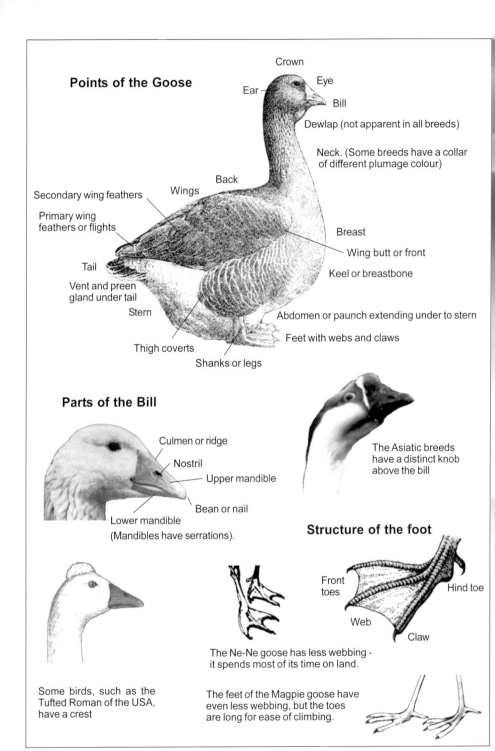

Points of the Goose

Crown

Eye

Ear

Bill

Dewlap (not apparent in all breeds)

Neck. (Some breeds have a collar of different plumage colour)

Back

Wings

Secondary wing feathers

Primary wing feathers or flights

Tail

Vent and preen gland under tail

Stern

Thigh coverts

Shanks or legs

Breast

Wing butt or front

Keel or breastbone

Abdomen or paunch extending under to stern

Feet with webs and claws

Parts of the Bill

Culmen or ridge

Nostril

Upper mandible

Bean or nail

Lower mandible
(Mandibles have serrations).

The Asiatic breeds have a distinct knob above the bill

Structure of the foot

Front toes

Hind toe

Web

Claw

The Ne-Ne goose has less webbing - it spends most of its time on land.

Some birds, such as the Tufted Roman of the USA, have a crest

The feet of the Magpie goose have even less webbing, but the toes are long for ease of climbing.

Domestic breeds of geese that are now recognised in Britain include African, American Buff, Brecon Buff, Buff Back, Chinese, Embden, Grey Back, Pilgrim, Pomeranian, Roman, Sebastopol, Steinbacher, Toulouse, and West of England.

In the USA, the following breeds are recognised: African, American Buff, Canada, Chinese, Egyptian, Embden, Pilgrim, Saddleback Pomeranian, Sebastopol, Toulouse, and Tufted Roman. Many other countries also have their own breed standards. There are variations between them.

Characteristics

Before taking a more detailed look at individual breeds, it is a good idea to examine the general characteristics of geese, always bearing in mind that there are variations from the norm. By looking at general characteristics, it is possible to provide conditions that are appropriate to the birds, taking into consideration their innate adaptations and needs.

Geese are large birds with long necks in relation to body length. This enables them to graze easily on land, as well as dredging water weeds in some cases. The bill is well adapted for grazing and snipping grasses because it has a row of serrations along the mandibles, which act like shears.

The legs of geese are more centrally placed than those of ducks, so walking on land is easier, again a factor that helps in grazing. The leg scales are reticulate (like a net) rather than the scutellate (shield-shaped) ones found in ducks. The feet are webbed for effective propulsion through the water, although breeds such as the Ne-Ne which spend most of their time on land, have less webbing. The tree-climbing Magpie goose has even less, but its toes are long for ease of climbing.

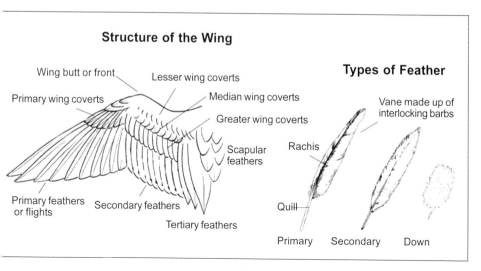

Structure of the Wing

Wing butt or front
Lesser wing coverts
Primary wing coverts
Median wing coverts
Greater wing coverts
Scapular feathers
Primary feathers or flights
Secondary feathers
Tertiary feathers

Types of Feather

Vane made up of interlocking barbs
Rachis
Quill
Primary   Secondary   Down

13

What a goose needs

 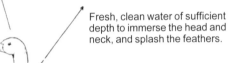

Good quality pasture with short-growing grasses, that is managed and used in rotation.

Fresh, clean water of sufficient depth to immerse the head and neck, and splash the feathers.

Dry, well ventilated shelter for night-time or bad weather protection, as well as anti-fox protection

Supplementary feed when grass has stopped growing, and at times such as breeding, rearing goslings or raising growers for the table.

Carrying a goose

Dealing with an aggressive gander

Make the hand and arm into an 'aggressive gander' and move it up and down in front of him until he backs away.

If he does not give way, make a quick circular motion of the hand, grab his neck and throw him off balance, but beware the strong wings!

If he is still aggressive - run and arm yourself with a dustbin lid shield next time!

Support the goose from below and in front, while keeping the wings confined against the body with your arm. A less tame goose may need to be carried with the head facing backwards.

Domestic geese (and all true geese) have one moult a year while sheldgeese are more like ducks in having two. Moulting is a natural process where old feathers are dropped, to be replaced by new ones. The external feathers are waterproofed by the preening action of the bird. This is where oil is transferred from the preen gland at the base of the tail to the plumage. The feathers are 'combed' at the same time so that the barbs on the vane of the feathers become interlocked, providing a smooth surface from which water is shed.

Geese are extremely hardy. The soft down feathers, under the waterproofed outer layer of plumage, provide an efficient layer of insulation that enables them to combat very cold weather. It is an attribute that has traditionally been made use of by man, in the manufacture of down pillows and duvets.

Behaviour

The sexes are generally (but not always) similar in plumage and show the same patterns of display. A female will adopt the same warning stance of outstretched neck and hissing noise as the gander, although he tends to be more aggressive, particularly in the breeding season.

Both sexes have the same vocal patterns which include hissing and honking. The gander, however, tends to go in for a spot of 'triumphalism' as well. This is where he 'sees off' a perceived threat, then runs back to the goose, with wings outstretched, proclaiming his success. She and others then join in the general clamour of triumph.

Most geese are fairly docile; it is their voluble honking and outstretched necks which frighten off those who are not familiar with the birds. There are times, such as the breeding season, however, when a gander can be aggressive, even to those who feed the flock. It is here that it is necessary for the feeder to try and imprint the notion of 'I can be aggressive too, so back off!'

As the diagrams opposite illustrate, making a 'goose-head and neck' shape with the hand and arm in front of the gander, can be effective. If this does not work, a more determined character can be thrown off balance by making a quick circular motion of the hand, then grabbing the neck and throwing him off balance. Beware of the strong wings, however! If all this fails, admit defeat and arm yourself with a dustbin lid shield next time you have to enter their enclosure!

Finally, it should be remembered that geese can be very long-lived; up to 40 years has been recorded. They can also adopt a monogamous attitude, with the gander sometimes chasing away a goose not of his choice. This is why it is important for newly introduced birds to have sufficient introductory time before the breeding season starts. In late winter, they form their breeding sets, and this is a much more straightforward business if they are all familiar with each other.

What to look for in a healthy goose

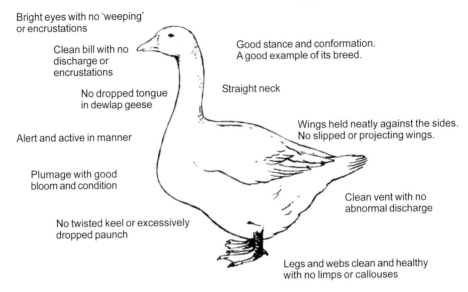

Bright eyes with no 'weeping' or encrustations

Clean bill with no discharge or encrustations

No dropped tongue in dewlap geese

Alert and active in manner

Plumage with good bloom and condition

No twisted keel or excessively dropped paunch

Good stance and conformation. A good example of its breed.

Straight neck

Wings held neatly against the sides. No slipped or projecting wings.

Clean vent with no abnormal discharge

Legs and webs clean and healthy with no limps or callouses

Choosing and buying stock

There are various options when it comes to buying geese, but the single most important advice is to obtain them from a breeder, rather than from an agent. Ideally, visit the farm where they have been raised so that you can see for yourself, the conditions that they enjoy. Most reputable breeders are only too pleased for you to do this, and will offer valuable advice on their care and management.

Secondly, buy the geese that are appropriate to your situation. If the main interest is in rearing for the Christmas market, it makes sense to obtain commercial strains or crosses. If pure breeds, for showing or for interest, are the priority, then consult the breed standards to ensure that they are good examples of their type. As referred to earlier, the BWA Standards provide excellent guidelines.

It goes without saying that the geese should be healthy and active. The drawing above indicates what to look out for in this respect.

The question then is at what age to buy? The choice is between adult birds, young growers, goslings or even fertile eggs. However, top breeders are unlikely to sell eggs or goslings, being more interested in selling adult birds. These will be more expensive and may not be the wisest purchase for a beginner. However, the advantage of adult birds is that they are hardy and may already be able to demonstrate their assets in terms of appearance or productivity. They will be the most expensive, particularly if they are recognised pure breeds. There may also be a waiting list for some breeds.

On guard duty at the farm gate. (Katie Thear)

Some breeders may be offering breeding pairs or trios (one male and two females). Here, it is important to establish their relationship, in case too much inbreeding results in future problems. Some prefer to obtain their ganders from a separate source. There is an advantage in buying a breeding set, however, and that is that the birds already recognise each other as part of the group, so there is unlikely to be a rejection problem at breeding time.

Young growers will be cheaper than adults, and they are also hardy. It is important to ensure that they come from a good breeding line. Ask for some information on this aspect. Pure bred stock may also be leg-ringed for identification.

Goslings are cheaper again, but will require protected conditions for they are not hardy. There are likely to be more casualties, and they are also at considerable risk from predators. They may not be sexed, so you may end up with more ganders than females.

Some breeders may sell fertile eggs. Here, an incubator and brooder are required, and the casualty rate is likely to be the highest. The hatchlings will need to be sexed at some point, and the surplus sold or raised for the domestic table.

Where small numbers are concerned, it is usually better to collect the birds yourself, for larger breeders may not deliver small consignments. If it is too far to the breeder's site, it may be possible to agree on a half-way point, or to meet up at a poultry and waterfowl show.

If the choice is to be a pure breed, ensure that birds are good examples of their type. All too often it is assumed that any large white goose is an Embden, while a small white goose is a Roman. To the uninitiated, this one could be mistaken for either, but in fact it is an Embden/Roman cross.

Birds that have already formed their breeding sets may be an easier option for the beginner because there will be no problem of rejection. (Katie Thear)

Breeds

Every goose after her kind. (Traditional saying)

The word 'geese' is a general term that encompasses a wide range of waterfowl, including domestic breeds and ornamental birds, as well as visiting migrants. The domestic breeds are also divided into heavy, medium and light classifications.

Domestic breeds

All the domestic breeds of geese were originally developed as utility birds for the farm, with an emphasis being placed on productivity in terms of growth for the table, egg production and feathers for bedding. In the last 150 years an emphasis has also been placed on the improvement of individual breeds, including the provision of standards which provide an ideal 'template' for each of the breeds. In more recent years, there has also been an emphasis on breeding for exhibition purposes. In some breeds, such as the Toulouse, there is now a marked difference between show and utility strains. As goose production has increased in the last few decades, commercial crosses and strains have also been developed.

Detailed descriptions and standards for all the recognised breeds of domestic geese are described in the *British Waterfowl Standards* published by the *British Waterfowl Association*. There are also descriptions in the *British Poultry Standards* produced by the *Poultry Club of Great Britain*, published by *Blackwells*. The standards for geese in the USA are included in the *American Standard of Perfection*, published by the *American Poultry Association*.

Heavy breeds

As the description implies, heavy breeds are the heaviest in weight, with some adult ganders weighing up to 12kg (26 lb) or more. Listed alphabetically, they are as follows:

African (See page 34)
This name is a misnomer as the breed is of Asian origin and, along with the Chinese breed to which it is related, originated in the Swatow area of China. Birds were exported to Britain and the USA during the early and mid-nineteenth century. There is some evidence that they were subsequently cross bred with the Chinese goose, which would have reduced their size. Traditionally, the favoured heavy breeds here were the European breeds, the Embden and the Toulouse.

Following imports of Africans from the United States to Britain during the 1980s, the size, standard and popularity of the breed has grown.

The African is a very large goose with good specimens attaining 90cm (3ft) in height. The body is well rounded with a large head and distinctive knob. The principal breed colour is brown (also known as grey) with the lower head, front of neck, breast and underbody being fawn to cream. There is a distinctive brown stripe from the crown to the bottom of the neck. The eyes are dark brown.

The body plumage feathers are brown edged with a lighter shading, the legs and webs are a deep orange and the eyes dark brown. The bill and knob are black. There are two other recognised colours: the Buff is marked similarly to the Brown but is lighter throughout, with a pinkish brown bill and knob. The legs and webs are light orange. The White variety has all-white plumage. The bill and knob are orange, the legs and webs are orange-yellow, and the eyes are blue.

Geese have large webbed feet on centrally-placed legs, so that walking on land is far easier for them than it is for ducks. This is an Embden. (Katie Thear)

The number of eggs laid in a season is around 15-25, but remember that, as with all breeds, there is a considerable variation depending on the individual strain. Wherever egg numbers are quoted, this factor should be borne in mind. Average weights are around 9kg (20lb) for a gander and 8kg (18lb) for a goose.

American Buff (See page 35)

The American Buff is a large goose developed in the United States from the Buff Saddleback Pomeranian. American breeders were keen to develop a heavy commercial meat bird, and it was finally standardised there in the 1940s. It is larger than the Brecon Buff, which it resembles.

The American Buff has a calm temperament, with a plump round body and a dual lobed paunch. The plumage is orange buff throughout, with feathers laced with a creamy white edging. The stern, paunch and tail are white. The bill, legs and webs are orange and eyes dark hazel. Weights are 11kg (24lb) for a gander and 9kg (20lb) for a goose. Eggs laid in a season are from 10-20.

Embden (See page 34)

The Embden originated in the German town of Emden where it seems to have been bred for at least the last 200 years. Imports into Britain from Germany and Holland led to crosses with English white geese during the nine-

A Grey Toulouse goose at ease in a pile of leaves in front of its house. This is the largest breed. (Katie Thear)

teenth century, producing a larger heavier bird. The first birds departed from the port of Bremen and the goose took this name before it finally resolved into Embden. (English spelling of the town of Emden at the time may have included a silent 'b').

The Embden has a large compact body with a strong neck and a dual lobed paunch. The tight feathered plumage is white throughout with orange bill, legs and webs, and blue eyes. Embdens grow rapidly and need plenty of exercise and not too much protein in their diet. Breeders particularly need to be prevented from becoming overweight as they need to be active. Such a large heavy bird can, when sitting, inadvertently break eggs or damage goslings so the use of a suitable incubator is advisable. Most (but not all) progeny are auto-sexing, with the females being darker than the males. Commercial weights can be 11kg (24lb) for a gander and 8kg (18lb) for a goose. Eggs laid in a season vary from 20-35.

The Toulouse lays more eggs, so a commercial bird can be raised by crossing an Embden gander with a Toulouse goose.

Toulouse (See page 35)

This is an old French breed and the largest goose. The original imports from France into Britain were crossed with the English Grey goose to increase the weight. In Britain there are now two distinct varieties, the Utility table bird and the exhibition Giant Dewlap bird. Similarly, in the United States, the Toulouse has two varieties: the Production Toulouse, and the Dewlap Toulouse.

Toulouse have a placid temperament, with a stately bearing, walking slowly around their domain without straying too far. They react to strangers with loud honkings and so make excellent watchdogs. They are unlikely to thrive during the spring and summer months on grass alone, so will need a supplementary feeding of pellets. It is important however, to make sure that they do not become too fat.

The Toulouse has a soft open plumage that cannot cope with periods of continuous rain, so bring them under cover if concerned. Having water to splash in will help them to keep their feathers clean and stimulate the preen gland, thus enabling them to oil and maintain the waterproof qualities of their plumage.

It has a broad deep shape and prominent breast. The neck, breast and keel are grey and the wings and thigh feathers are grey edged with white. The stern, paunch and tail are white. The legs, webs and feet are orange and the eyes dark brown. There are two lesser known colour varieties, the Buff which is identical to the standard grey but with the grey replaced with buff, and the White which is an all white bird with blue eyes. A commercial Toulouse can finish at 12kg (26lb) for a gander and 9kg (20lb) for a goose. Eggs laid in a season vary between 30-50.

Medium breeds

As the name suggests, these are slightly smaller breeds of domestic geese.

Brecon Buff (See page 38)

This breed originated in the uplands of Wales when Rhys Llewelyn from Swansea purchased a number of buff geese from upland farms in the Brecon Beacons during the late 1920s and early 1930s. He began breeding with an Embden gander but by 1934 was breeding all-buff birds and had published his own breed standard. His aim was to produce a sturdy table goose that was economical to raise and could thrive in upland conditions.

Buffs are indeed hardy, of good temperament and excellent converters of food into meat; better than most of the heavy breeds.

The Brecon Buff has a broad compact and rounded body shape and a dual paunch. It should be a deep shade of buff all over, with the bill, legs and feet pink and the eyes dark brown. As pink is recessive to orange, orange-pink legs and feet are quite common. Eggs laid in a season vary from 20-40. Adult weights are 8kg (18lb) for a gander and 7kg (16lb) for a goose.

Brecon Buffs in front of their open-fronted barn. Straw has been placed on the ground immediately in front of this to prevent muddy conditions. Note the heavy-based feeder on the right. (Katie Thear)

Buff Back (See page 38)

The Buff Back, like the Grey Back and Pomeranian, is a white goose with coloured neck and saddleback markings. These distinctive markings may have been derived from buff marked Pomeranians or cross bred from white and buff geese. Like all saddlebacks, its origins lie in Northern Europe. It has a long plump body with a double lobed paunch. The head, upper neck, back and thigh coverts are buff with white lacing of the feathers. The remainder of the body is white. The bill, legs and webs are orange and the eyes blue. Adult weights are around 9kg (20lb) for a gander and 8kg (18lb) for a goose.

Grey Back (See page 38)

The Grey Back is a Northern European goose with similar shape and markings to the Buff Back except that buff is replaced by grey.

Pomeranian (See page 39)

Grey backed Pomeranian geese originated in the Pomeranian region of north eastern Germany. It is a hardy bird with good fertility and similar in markings to British saddleback geese, with a long body and full breast and shoulders giving a characteristic egg shape, with a single paunch. The head, upper neck and thigh

A pair of Buff Backs enjoying the extensive lawns of a large garden. (Katie Thear)

coverts are dark grey edged with white. The remainder of the body is white. The bill is orange-pink and the legs and feet orange-red. Pomeranians are good layers producing around 20-50 eggs per season. Adult weights are around 9kg (20lb) for ganders and 8kg (18lb) for geese.

West of England (See page 38)

Like the Pilgrim and Shetland, the West of England goose is a sex linked breed which breeders have saved from decline, and is probably a descendent of the early farmyard goose, once common throughout the country before the importation of heavy breeds from the Continent. There is a similar breed in Normandy which is also of ancient lineage. (See Normandy goose on page 30).

The breed has a longish body with a broad back and dual paunch. The gander is white and the goose has a grey and white head and neck, the breast and flanks are white and the remainder is grey with white laced feathers on the coverts and scapulars. The tail is white with some grey feathers. In both sexes the bill is orange and the legs and webs orange or pink. Eyes are blue. Adult weights are 8kg (18lb) for a gander and 7kg (15lb) for a goose.

Brown (or Grey) Chinese geese at an agricultural show. (Katie Thear)

White Chinese geese. The Asiatic breeds all have a prominent knob above the bill.

Light Breeds

The smallest of the goose breeds, these are active birds, and are frequently good egg layers.

Chinese (See page 42)
Like the African breed, the Chinese came from China and originated from the wild Swan goose. The first birds were imported into Britain and the USA in the mid-nineteenth century. Subsequently, most interest was shown in the heavier breeds and it was not until the 1930s that interest in the Chinese was stimulated again. Today they are very popular and make excellent watchdogs. The meat is darker than most geese but it has a good flavour. They do not fatten well, however, and butchers may be unwilling to take them, but they are fine for eating at home.

The Brown (Grey) Chinese has an upright stance with a long neck and a short compact body. There is a pronounced knob at the top of the bill. The lower part of the head, front of neck and breast are light fawn. There is a dark brown stripe extending from the crown to the back of the neck. Sides and coverts are grey brown with light edging and the wings have laced feathering varying from dark slate to grey brown. The tail coverts and stern are white. The bill and knob are black, legs and webs orange and eyes dark brown.

The White Chinese has all-white plumage with an orange bill and knob, orange yellow legs and webs and blue eyes. Chinese geese are good layers producing 50-70 eggs per season. Adult weights are 5kg (11lb) for a gander and 4kg (9lb) for a goose.

Pilgrim (See page 43)

The Pilgrim breed almost certainly originated in Britain, but was first standardised in the United States. Like the West of England and Shetland breeds, it is auto-sexing with white males and grey and white females. Such geese were common in farmyards around Britain until the popularity of the imported Embden and Toulouse, and the developments arising from these breeds, displaced them. It is highly likely that these traditional farm-yard geese were among the livestock that travelled to America with the early Pilgrims, but, as in Europe, they prac-

Roman geese are small and some may have head crests, like the one at the back. (Katie Thear)

tically died out with the imports of heavier breeds.

In the USA, the Pilgrim was re-developed as an auto-sexing breed and first standardised in 1939 from European genetic material. However, Pilgrim geese in the UK have been bred here from indigenous stock and not imported from the USA. The Pilgrim has a plump, meaty body with a double-lobed paunch. The gander is pure white and the goose is light grey with darker grey wings and a white stern. There is some white around the eye and on the face. In both sexes the bill, legs and webs are orange. The eyes are blue-grey in the gander and hazel brown in the goose. Adult weights are 7kg (15lb) for a gander and 6kg (13lb) for a goose.

Roman (See page 42)

The history of this little white goose is unclear, except that like all European geese it originated from the Greylag. The Roman goose was around in ancient Rome, according to accounts from that period, and a similar goose seems to have become widely disseminated in southern and Eastern Europe. Reference has already been made to the fact that white geese were herded over the Alps to Rome.

Romans are lively little geese with an even temperament, and one gander can be kept with as many as five females. Although similar in colouring to the Embden, they are of quite a different size and shape with shorter necks and legs. They were first imported into Britain and the USA in the early part of the twentieth century and today have a strong following among a number of breeders. The Roman is all-white with sleek plumage and a plump, compact, deep body. The bill, legs and webs are orange pink and the eyes blue. Some Romans, particularly those in America, have a small head crest. In fact, the USA Standards require there to be a crest. It is a good laying breed producing around 30-60 eggs in a season. Adult weights are around 6kg (13lb) for a gander and 5kg (11lb) for a goose.

Sebastopol (See page 43)

Sebastopol geese originated around the Black Sea and the lower reaches of the Danube. Their most distinctive feature is their curled or frizzled feathers. This mutation was selected for, as curled feathers make the best down stuffing for pillows. They were imported into Britain and the USA in the mid-nineteenth century and have since been developed into a larger bird.

Although they are kept here mostly as ornamental birds, they have good utility qualities, being reasonable layers and are able to put on weight well. They should not be kept with other breeds as damage can occur to feathers from vigorous behaviour. Like all geese, they should have enough water to splash in, in order to keep their feathers clean. In Britain there are two types, the Frizzle and the Smooth-Breasted. Both types have the same general shape, being short, round-backed birds on short legs. The Frizzle has smooth feathers on the head and upper neck and curled feathers everywhere else. Those covering the wings and back are longer and almost touch the ground, practically hiding the legs and feet.

The Smooth-Breasted type is much the same except that it has smooth feathers on the breast, belly and paunch in addition to the head and neck. In the USA, only geese with bodies that are entirely covered by frizzled feathers are acceptable.

There are also two recognised colours here. Although most Sebastopols are all-white, there is a Buff version where the plumage is all-buff. In both colours and types the bill, legs and webs are orange. Eyes are blue in the white variety and brown in the buff. Sebastopols can lay around 25-35 eggs in a season. Adult weights are around 6.5kg (14lb) for the male and 5.5kg (12lb) for a goose.

Shetland (See page 43)

This is a smaller variety of the West of England goose with the same feature of being auto-sexing, and having an all-white gander and a grey and white goose.

Steinbacher (See page 42)

Goose fighting used to be popular in Eastern Europe, Russia and China, and breeds were selected for this purpose. The German fighting goose, bred from a cross between Chinese and local farm geese, comes from the Steinbach area of Germany but it is now kept primarily as an ornamental variety.

The Steinbacher goose was originally imported into Britain in the 1980s and is in fact quite tame. They are hardy birds, and grow well. The Steinbacher is a fine strong looking goose with a wide back and breast, tight plumage and long wings. There is a light dual paunch on older birds. The striking feature of the Steinbacher is the blue colour. It is the only blue goose and is blue grey with light lacing throughout, and with laced grey tail feathers. The bill is orange with a black bean at the tip. Legs and webs are also orange and the eyes are dark brown. There are other colour varieties on the Continent. Steinbachers lay 20-35 eggs in a season. Adult weights are 6.5kg (14lb) for the male and 5.5kg (12lb) for a goose.

Other domestic breeds

There are other breeds of domestic geese, of course, with many European countries having their own types and strains that have been developed for various markets. These are obviously not recognised in the BWA Standards while they are not here in any numbers, but many have Standards in their own countries, as for example the *Fédération Française et la Commission des Standards* of France.

Alsatian (L'oie d'Alsace)
The Alsatian or Alsace is a small, white goose that was bred in the Alsace area of France for the production of liver paté de foie gras. It has short legs and a particularly wide body to provide the maximum area for enlargement of the liver. The unpleasant practice of force-feeding geese in order to produce large, fatty livers, is legal in France but not in Britain, although the paté is imported here.

Arsamas
This is one of the fighting geese of Russia, named after the town of Arsamas in the province of Nizhny-Novgorod. An all-white goose, similar to the Embden, it is a heavy breed with a curved bill. The practice of goose fighting was officially banned at the beginning of the last century, although it still continues in remote areas.

Benkovski
This is the main goose breed of Bulgaria. Bred from Embdens and Toulouse crossed with local geese of the area, they are also used for the production of enlarged livers for paté production.

Bohemian
The Czech republic and the surrounding area are credited with this white, medium-sized breed. In the 19th century, larger geese were imported for crossing with them, but the *Bohemian Geese Club* still maintains a small number of the original type.

Bresse (L'oie de Bresse or l'oie de l'Ain)
A medium weight breed, this white goose suffers from never having had a recognised standard. It is a smaller, active version of the White Bourbonnais, but existing flocks show too great a variety of characteristics to make a standard possible.

Celler
This is a medium weight, buff coloured goose from the Hanover area of Germany.

Diepholz
Originating in the Diepholz area of Northern Germany, this is an all-white, light breed that is closely related to the farmyard grey goose. It has been bred for well over a hundred years in the area, and was recognised by the German Standards in 1925. It is also found in Switzerland.

Flamande (L'oie Flamande)

A medium sized goose, this French breed is recognised in two varieties, the White and the Grey and White.

French Toulouse (Toulouse Francaise)

There are two versions of this heavy breed: the Dewlapped Toulouse (L'oie de Toulouse à Bavette) and the smaller Toulouse Agricole version without a dewlap (L'oie de Toulouse sans Bavette). Both versions originated in the Toulouse area of France, but the dewlapped strain was selectively bred for size by English breeders and then reintroduced to France. As in Britain, this is now regarded as a show breed, while the non-dewlapped strain is primarily a farmyard bird.

Grey Landes (L'oie Gris des Landes)

Originating in Landes, in the south-east of France, this grey breed was developed from the Toulouse in order to produce a lighter goose for paté de foie gras. In recent years, it has also been selectively bred for commercial use so that strains of Grey Landes are now one of the most common, commercial geese in France.

Gruse of the Poitou Marshes (L'oie Grise du Marais Poitevin)

The marshes of western Poitou in France traditionally had flocks of these beautiful grey geese. People living there had the right to graze a 'barrel' on the communal area. A 'barrel' was defined as two ganders, nine geese and any resulting goslings. The latter were raised for roasting and for feather and down production. In 1992 there were only two breeders left and action was taken to preserve the breed in its original area. A breeding programme according to the standards was instigated and since then, the numbers have increased.

Kholmogory

This is the largest of the Russian fighting geese, and was bred by crossing the Chinese with local geese of the Central Chernozem region. It has the distinctive bill knob of the Asiatic geese and is found in three varieties: the White, Grey and the Grey and White. Unlike the other fighting goose breeds, this seems to have been produced exclusively for fighting, with little evidence of its having been reared for the table or for feather and down production in the past. More recently, however, it was crossed with other domestic breeds such as the Embden, to produce the Kholmogorsk for commercial production. As a result, many flocks now have birds without the characteristic knob.

Magyar

As the name suggests, this is the white goose of Hungary. An ancient breed, it was known to the Romans, and may well have the same origin as the Roman goose. These days, it has been used to produce a number of hybridised, commercial strains for higher egg yield, table and liver production.

Russian Fighting Geese

Arsamas   Kholmogory   Tula

Meusian (L'oie de la Meuse)
Conservation came too late for this small, grey goose of the Meuse river area of France and Belgium. No-one, as yet, has been able to find examples and it is probably extinct. It was like a small, grey version of the Alsatian goose.

Normandy (L'oie Normande)
Bred in Normandy from local geese of the area, this medium-sized goose is similar to our West of England. It is an auto-sexing breed in that males and females can be identified at hatching. The adult gander is all-white while the females are grey and white.

Oland
This is a rare breed named after the island of Oland in Sweden. It is a fairly short-legged, white and grey-backed bird.

Touraine (L'oie de Touraine)
A breed that is similar to the White Bourbonnais and White Poitou, this breed differs from both in having a longer neck. It has all-white plumage with yellow-orange bill and legs. Developed as a table goose, as well as a feather and down producer, it is characterised by its rapid development and hardiness. Unfortunately, it has never been standardised.

Tula
Another of the Russian fighting geese, this is named after the town of the same name. It is a large, grey goose with a curved bill, but there is also a brown variety.

White Bourbonnais (L'oie blanche du Bourbonnais)
This breed originated in the department of Allier in France. It is a large, all-white goose with a reputation for hardiness and good egg production. The females are

Grey geese, such as these belonging to the author, have been used in commercial crosses, but in the UK they are not as popular as white. (Brian Hale)

also said to be good brooders and mothers. Its development was mainly to produce good-sized roasting geese. There are several varieties but only one, the all-white with red-orange bill, is recognised.

White Poitou (L'oie Blanche du Poitou)
An all-white goose, this breed is said to have been introduced to Poitiers by a group of Dutch people who had settled there under the auspices of the Duke of Aquitaine. It is fairly small without much of a paunch, and has blue eyes and orange legs and webs. Bred for the table and for its feathers and down, the White Poitou was also distinguished for its skin production. This was where sections of skin with down were sold as 'swan strips' or powder puffs.

Xupu
Named after the area of Xupu in the Hunan province of China, this is a medium weight, white Chinese goose with the typical knob on the bill. Some are distinctive for also having crested heads.

Yane
From the Anjui province of China, these are grey Chinese geese with the typical knobbed bills. They are regarded as heavy geese on account of their large size.

Commercial geese

Although geese have not been as intensively bred as chickens, there are a number of companies which have specialised in developing birds that are efficient meat producers, with a good meat to bone ratio, as well as economic feed conversion. These are the best choice for the commercial producer for they can be raised to the right weight range that the

Legarth geese, the leading commercial strain from Denmark. (Goose Producers' Association)

market demands. These days, commercial flocks of geese are almost invariably hybrid strains which have been selected for good growth, prolific egg production and general hardiness. Many of them come from Scandinavian sources.

Legarth

Legarths are all-white geese which originated in Denmark where they have been developed for commercial use in *Bulow's Hatchery*. They have long, broad breasts and have an average growth rate of 7.2 kilos in 14 weeks. They are now the most common strain for commercial use in Britain

Grey Landes

Referred to earlier, the Grey Landes has also been selectively bred for commercial use and is now one of the most common, commercial breeds in France.

In addition to these, there are of course, many other commercial strains of geese which have been developed over the years, and have been given names that reflect the area of origin. In more recent years, strains of these geese may also have been given specific names by their particular breeders.

Generally speaking, most of the commercial breed strains have been developed from one or more of the following: Embden, Chinese and Toulouse. The Chinese gives a higher egg production rate, while the Toulouse provides increased body weight. The Embden contributes a good body weight as well as white feathers. Most producers of table geese in Britain prefer white-feathered birds to grey-feathered ones.

Housing

Even a shed that is a long way from the pastures can be used, for geese are easily driven and soon learn to find their way about.
(L.C. Turnill, 1944)

Housing needs are simple and, depending on the numbers, can be anything from a shed or outbuilding to a stable or barn. The key requirements are a dry interior with plenty of ventilation. It is also useful to think of housing in terms of both night-time shelter and day-time shade or other protection.

Geese are cool weather birds and pretty hardy. Apart from wind which they really do not like, they prefer to be in the open all the time. However, when the temperature climbs above 21C, they need to be able to find some shade. We had large mature trees growing all around and within our pasture so there were several areas at any time of the day in shade. If this natural cover is not available, then temporary shelter can easily be constructed using straw bales as two walls and old doors or corrugated iron sheets for a roof. Make sure that there is a good flow of air through it. Such a construction can also be employed as a shelter from the wind during windy periods, although this version would need three sides. (See illustration on page 36).

To protect the flock from night attacks from foxes, it is necessary to shut them up in secure housing. The fox often comes at dusk and at dawn so make sure that they go in early and are not let out until it is quite light. Make certain that the house is secure. Wire over windows, and reinforce any weak points at ground level. It is essential for the health of the geese that the house is well ventilated and there should be a minimum ground area of 0.7 - 0.9 sq.m (7.5 - 10 sq.ft) per bird. A largely open-sided house is fine provided that it faces away from the wind and that the opening is covered with strong mesh. However, in an open-sided house with a mesh wall, have a drop-down cover available for when winter winds change direction and an icy Siberian gale howls in from the east.

If you are fortunate enough to have barns or other farm buildings, these can easily be adapted for geese. For a small flock, an inexpensive garden shed is also suitable, as long as the glass window is removed and replaced with strong mesh. There are also purpose-made goose houses available from a number of manufacturers and suppliers.

If there are badgers around, make sure that the housing is robust and badger-proof. Badgers are strong animals and can cause a lot of damage to housing. Goslings are also at risk from them. (Continued on page 36)

Heavy Breeds of Domestic Geese

Brown African geese. (John Tarren).

White African. (John Tarren)

Embden. (Katie Thear)

Production or Utility Toulouse.
This does not have the large dewlap which is found in the Exhibition Toulouse shown below.

(American Livestock Breeds Conservancy)

American Buff. (John Tarren)

Exhibition Buff Toulouse. (John Tarren)

Exhibition Grey Toulouse. (John Tarren)

Examples of goose housing and shelters

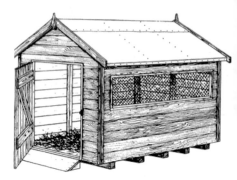

An open-fronted house with wire netting on the door and one wall, to provide good ventilation. The small section of verandah roof provides extra weather protection.

Here, a garden shed has had the windows removed and replaced with wire netting. There is also a ramp provided for ease of going in and out.

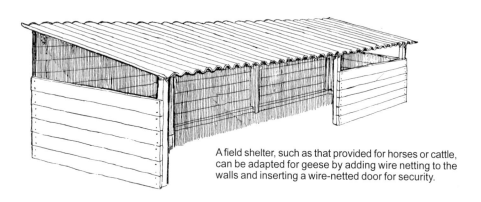

A field shelter, such as that provided for horses or cattle, can be adapted for geese by adding wire netting to the walls and inserting a wire-netted door for security.

Straw bales and a sheet of corrugated iron can be used to make a temporary shade or other shelter.

If a goose is sitting on a clutch of eggs outside, it may be easier to construct a shelter around her, rather than trying to move her.

A small goose shelter for this breeding group of Toulouse geese. The entrance and vents provide ventilation, while the roof is slanted backwards so that rainwater is shed away from the entrance. There is no door here because the enclosure fencing is fox-proof. (Katie Thear)

Whether you are housing geese or goslings, the house must be wholly mink and rat-proof. As well as attacking goslings, rats also contaminate feedstuffs, and spread disease.

Some ornamental breeds of geese may need extra winter protection such as a large aviary.

Yard

If you are bringing your geese off pasture and into a secure yard at night, the same precautions are necessary with regard to wind, weather and fox protection. If they are spending some time in the yard you will need to provide 2.3 - 4.6 sq.m (25 - 50 sq ft) per bird, and the ground will need to be free of mud and stagnant water.

In a yard or field be aware of nearby trees with branches that could provide an entry point for outside predators. If in doubt, cut them back. Geese need to keep their feathers reasonably clean in order to survive harsh weather conditions, so ensure that house or yard has a good bed of straw, and add to it as required. As well as straw or chopped straw (which is preferable as it does not compact) baled, untreated wood shavings are suitable for bedding. Soiled bedding can be removed and composted with other compost material and garden waste. The resulting compost should not be put back on the pasture, as parasites can endure and be picked up. It can be put to good use in the kitchen garden.

(Continued on page 40)

Medium Breeds of Domestic Geese

Grey Back. (John Tarren)

West of England. (John Tarren)

Buff Back. (Katie Thear)

Brecon Buff. (John Tarren)

Pomeranian and a regular 'Best of breed' winner at the BWA national championship, as well as being the Reserve Champion at the Poultry Club National Show, 1998. (Jenny Pritchard).

Anti-fox perimeter fencing

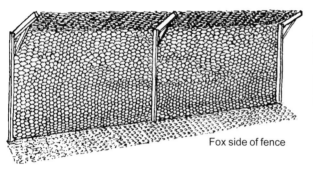

Fox side of fence

A 2m (6.5ft) high perimeter fence with an extra 30cm (12in) overhang to deter climbing over. The netting is well dug in to prevent burrowing under. If this type of fencing is not available, electric fencing can be used.

Electric fencing

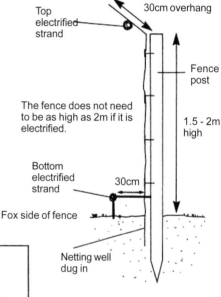

Top electrified strand

30cm overhang

Fence post

The fence does not need to be as high as 2m if it is electrified.

1.5 - 2m high

Bottom electrified strand

30cm

Fox side of fence

Netting well dug in

Goose predator number one

The fox, *Vulpes vulpes*, is capable of taking an adult goose. The presence of a gander is not an effective protection, as some have found to their cost.

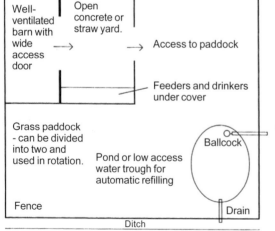

Well-ventilated barn with wide access door

Open concrete or straw yard.

→   →   Access to paddock

Feeders and drinkers under cover

Grass paddock - can be divided into two and used in rotation.

Pond or low access water trough for automatic refilling

Ballcock

Water in

Fence

Drain

Ditch

A house and yard used in conjunction with pasture

Pasture

Young fresh grass is a very nutritious food, but as it becomes mature so its value deteriorates. (Leonard Robinson, 1948)

Geese are grazing birds and from spring, through summer and early autumn, they can obtain much of their food requirements from grass. If you do not have access to grass then keeping geese is not a practical option.

Ideally grazing for geese should be no more than 10 cm (4 in) high and consist of fresh young grasses. These contain nutrients missing from more tough and fibrous vegetation. Particularly narrow leaved and shallow rooted grasses are not really suitable as they are likely to become tough and wiry. Tough fibrous material can lead to digestive impaction and constipation. An ideal mixture for geese would be perennial ryegrass, timothy and clover.

Traditionally geese were grazed on large areas of common land and along roadsides where there was a varied mixture of herbs and grasses. If your pasture has grown long, you can put animals such as cattle or sheep onto it beforehand, and the geese can then follow on. Alternatively, you can mow it for them.

Geese have ribbed margins on their bills, with a series of sharp points like teeth and this is an ideal tool for cutting grass very low. Indeed it is said that you can follow cattle with sheep as there is sufficient length of grass left behind, but geese like sheep, leave nothing to eat on well grazed land until it grows on.

In Britain, grass loses its protein and vitamin values steadily throughout the summer months, so by autumn supplementary feeding will need to be increased. During the spring and summer they can obtain most if not all their nutritional needs from grass and will only need access to fresh water and grit, but much depends on the quality of grass and the age of the geese. (See Feeding).

An orchard is an ideal environment for geese as they prefer the shade in mid-summer and the grasses will grow lush and green under those conditions. Geese will keep the orchard trimmed and tidy and will also clear away any windfalls. Geese will however damage the trunks of young trees by stripping the new bark, so these will need wire protection. If there are any plants or trees which are poisonous they should be fenced off or removed. However, most animals will not eat poisonous plants. Yew can be dangerous but we had extensive yew hedges and no problems. We did however cut down a Laburnum. Other plants to avoid are Deadly Nightshade, Hemlock and Foxgloves.

(Continued on page 44)

Light Breeds of Domestic Geese

White Chinese. (John Tarren)

Brown (or Grey) Chinese. (John Tarren)

Steinbacher. (John Tarren)

Roman. (John Tarren)

Pilgrim goose. As with the West of England and Shetland, the female is grey and white, while the gander is all-white. (Katie Thear)

A pair of Shetlands with the gander on the left. It is a smaller version of the West of England. (Katie Thear)

A Champion Sebastopol at the National Poultry Show. (Katie Thear)

An example of rotation of pasture for breeders and growers

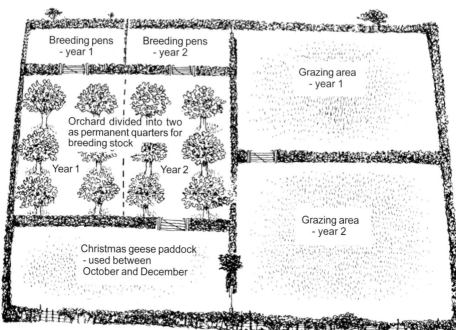

This system is just one of many alternatives, depending on individual situation and nature of the enterprise. The key factor with any system is to ensure that pasture is rotated regularly, with young stock always having the first choice of grass.

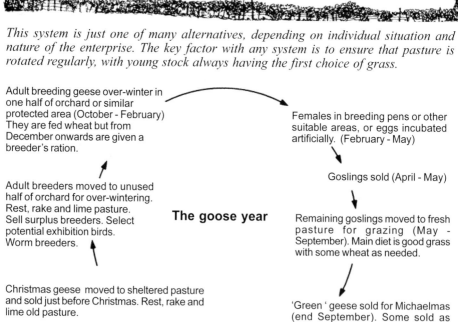

Adult breeding geese over-winter in one half of orchard or similar protected area (October - February) They are fed wheat but from December onwards are given a breeder's ration.

Females in breeding pens or other suitable areas, or eggs incubated artificially. (February - May)

Goslings sold (April - May)

Adult breeders moved to unused half of orchard for over-wintering. Rest, rake and lime pasture. Sell surplus breeders. Select potential exhibition birds. Worm breeders.

The goose year

Remaining goslings moved to fresh pasture for grazing (May - September). Main diet is good grass with some wheat as needed.

Christmas geese moved to sheltered pasture and sold just before Christmas. Rest, rake and lime old pasture.

'Green ' geese sold for Michaelmas (end September). Some sold as potential breeders or exhibition birds.

Protection against predators

Many people believe that a gander is capable of seeing off a fox, but I'm afraid that this is not true. One of our geese was taken by a fox one night, but we were warned by the sounds of alarm and rushed out with Sandy the dog. There was Reynard trying to pull a goose through the hedge, while the gander was lying low and keeping out of it. Fortunately the fox dropped the goose and ran when it saw Sandy, and we were able to retrieve the goose. She had a nasty wound on her neck and had lost quite a few feathers, but she made a good recovery and lived for many years to tell her goslings the tale of the night of the fox.

There are only two effective ways of keeping out a fox: having fences that cannot be scaled or having an electric fence. Our local hunt was concerned only with chasing foxes for pleasure. They were quite useless at reducing the fox population, and in our experience, caused damage when the hounds rampaged across our land in an uncontrolled way.

A fence needs to be 2m (6.5ft) high, well dug into the ground to prevent burrowing under, and preferably with an extra 30cm (1ft) overhang angled outwards, to keep out foxes. (See the diagrams on page 40).

Fences that are lower than this can be made safe by being electrified. This is a matter of running a wire along the top and bottom of the fence, but around 30cm (1ft) out from it on the fox side. (See page 40). Suppliers of electric fencing have a range of suitable systems and will normally advise on specific situations.

Stocking densities

The amount of pasture you need will vary with the quality of grasses and climatic conditions. It is also important to distinguish between permanent breeding stock and table growers. The latter will be occupying pasture for a limited period so the stocking density will be higher than it is for breeders which are kept on a permanent basis. As a general guideline, the following are the maximum stated densities for organically raised geese, but again it must be emphasised that the nature and quality of the pasture ultimately dictate what density is suitable.

> Heavy breeding stock – 12 birds per hectare (5 per acre).
> Light breeders – 15 birds per hectare (6 per acre).
> Growers or market geese – 600 birds per hectare (250 per acre).

Rotation of pasture

Pasture needs to be used in rotation so that it has a resting period before being used again. Over-use of pasture can lead to a build-up of gizzard worm, a parasite that has a particularly debilitating effect on young stock. They should always be raised on clean, fresh pasture. (Continued on page 48)

Ornamental Breeds of Geese

Lesser White-Fronted goose. (Katie Thear)

Red-Breasted goose. (Katie Thear)

Ne-Ne or Hawaian goose. (Katie Thear)

Canada goose. (Clipart Collection)

Bar-Headed Goose. (Katie Thear)   Emperor geese. (Katie Thear)

Three Barnacle geese and an Emperor goose at the back. (Katie Thear)

47

The diagrams on page 44 show one system that caters for both breeders and growers, but there are many different alternatives, depending on the individual site.

In this system, the breeding birds are over-wintered in one half of an orchard where there is a house and wind protection from the trees. A bank of breeding pens is made available when breeding is seen to be commencing. These may need to be sub-divided where different breeds are kept, in order to avoid inter-breeding. Where the geese are all one breed, the pens may simply be a bank of nesting areas where, hopefully, the females will lay and hatch their eggs, as well as brood their goslings. Alternatively, the eggs can be removed for artificial incubation. (This will encourage the laying of more eggs).

Once the goslings are hardy, they are allowed to access the main grazing area. The breeders can, if necessary follow on after them, so that the young birds always have first choice of the best grass. Some of the growers may be sold as 'green' geese for Michaelmas, as indicated in the 'goose year' diagram on page 44. As the grass declines, the growers are moved to a new and protected area of pasture where they can be given supplementary feeding to make up for the deficit of nutrients in the grass. Those destined for the table are then killed just before Christmas. Some may be sold as prospective breeding stock or exhibition birds if they are good examples of the relevant pure breeds.

The breeders are given access to their next over-wintering quarters, in this case, the second half of the orchard. Before this move, it is an appropriate time to administer a wormer such as *Flubenvet* in the feed. (See the Health section).

Care and maintenance of pasture

Vacated pasture areas need to be rested and raked. Depending on the size of paddocks, and the equipment available, this will be done by tractor with a harrow attachment or with a hand rake. The process helps to disperse any areas of compacted droppings. It also scarifies the grass, opening it up to increased aeration as well as uprooting pasture weeds.

Now is also a good time to lime the land, particularly if it is heavy or acidic. A sample of the soil can easily be taken in order to test its pH (positive hydrogen) value. A reading will indicate the level of acidity or alkalinity. Good pasture land will have a reading of between 5.5 to 6.5pH. Soil testing kits are widely available in garden centres.

An application of lime helps to flocculate the clay particles in heavy clay, improving the texture and drainage of the soil. It also unlocks other soil elements, making them available to the grasses. Traditionally, lime is said to have a 'sweetening' effect on pasture. It also helps to disperse any residual parasites. The application rate is around 0.25kg (0.5lb) per 0.8 sq.m (1 sq. yd).

A family group of farmyard geese on pasture. (Martin Lynch).

Where the ground is very waterlogged, it may need to be drained. On a small scale, this may simply be a case of digging a hole and filling it with clinker so that surplus water collects there rather than lying on the surface. On a larger scale, It may be a case of breaking up the surface 'pan' or compaction, digging some trenches and inserting drainage pipes. Contractors will do this if required.

Leaving the ground fallow (no stock on it) also breaks the life cycle of parasites which need to have hosts in order to complete their development. If the ground is known to have a heavy burden of parasites, and their associated intermediate hosts, slugs and snails, it may be a good idea to disperse them by applying the following mixture: 1 part copper sulphate mixed with 6 parts sand applied at the rate of 0.45kg (1lb) per 0.83 sq.m (1 sq.yd). On a larger scale, the application rate is 254 kg (5 cwt) per 0.4 hectare (1 acre).

If the pasture is looking a bit patchy, bare areas can be resown during the fallow period. A good quality ley mixture containing perennial ryegrass, white clover, meadow grasses and fescues is suitable. Don't buy lawn grass seed from garden shops. Get a proper agricultural mix from a specialist supplier who will have a range of modern varieties that are suitable for grazing geese. Around 50g is enough for one square metre (500kg per hectare). If the grass needs feeding, a good, safe fertilizer to use is calcified seaweed.

Water

Geese obviously need access to fresh drinking water at all times, but what about access to water for swimming or splashing?

Like all waterfowl, geese love a pond where they can splash, swim and keep their feathers clean. It is said by many breeders that having access to a pond aids fertility and mating, and certainly some of the heavyweights such as exhibition Toulouse, might find it difficult to mate without the help of water.

Domestic geese generally spend far more of their time on grass than ducks. Our ducks would rush for the pond as soon as they were let out in the morning, but the geese would remain on pasture most of the time, only occasionally taking a quick dip in the pond.

Many breeders provide splashing rather than swimming facilities. This allows the geese to immerse their heads and splash water over their feathers. The pond shown on the right has a ballcock attachment to allow for automatic refilling so that there is always fresh water available. It also has the advantage of being moveable so that it can accompany the geese when they are moved to fresh pasture. It is available from poultry equipment suppliers.

For a small number of geese, a simple way of providing splashing water is to use a large plastic washing up bowl. This can be placed in an old tyre to stop it being tipped over. The advantage of doing this is that the bowl is easily emptied, washed out and refilled with a hose, and it can be moved around easily so that muddy patches do not build up. An old sink or suitably large and robust container, can also be used but will need to be constantly emptied and refilled, so make sure that this can be done without too much difficulty.

Ponds and streams

If you are fortunate enough to have a stream running through your land then you have potentially ideal conditions for keeping waterfowl. Even a slow moving stream, providing it does not dry up in summer, can be partially dammed to make a pond with flowing water which will be continuously refreshed, washing away mud and excrement downstream. However, before attempting any construction ensure that you are aware of the likely maximum and minimum depth of your stream during the year. Recent years have shown that there are more concentrated periods of rainfall than in the past. Under these circumstances a stream or river can rise rapidly within hours so make sure that you are fully prepared. If you are keeping different breeds and there is sufficient water flow, you can fence off separate areas for each breed in the stream.

Instead of damming the stream itelf, it is possible to construct a pond and divert stream water into it, closing the inlet when full. To clean it, you open an exit

A moveable splashing pond with an automatic ballcock for keeping it refilled. The run-off goes into a small stream. These are Sebastopols whose long frizzled feathers need to be kept clean. (Katie Thear)

so that the water can flow away downstream. Fresh stream water can be allowed to flow through until it is fully flushed out. Then, it can be refilled. However, do check that there are no septic tanks emptying into the water upstream. Such pollutants can infect the goose eggs. If you are concerned you can arrange to have a bacteriological test carried out. You can also have a water sample tested for a small fee.

Even without an existing water course you may still wish to have a pond. Before you begin, consider how it can be periodically drained and cleaned. By using a flexible butyl liner you can position your pond on sloping ground with a water hose inlet at the top end and an outlet at the bottom end with a pipe to drain the water away. These can be partially opened to achieve a throughflow. Plastic or light-duty butyls are not recommended, for they can tear too easily. Heavy-duty butyl is quite different and is now widely used.

The larger the pond, the longer it will take to drain and refill. Ideally a pond should not be sited beneath overhanging trees which will deposit large numbers of leaves into it in the autumn. If the surface area is large enough, the pond will receive sufficient aeration from the air, particularly if the water is being agitated regularly by swimming geese. For this type of balanced, natural aeration, the surface area needs to be around ten times the depth of the pond. Smaller ponds may need to have a pump to do the job.

If you are planning to construct a permanent pond that can only be cleaned out occasionally, you will need 5 sq.m (50 sq.ft) per goose and a minimum depth of 60cms (2 ft). However, if possible it should be deeper so that sediment on the bottom is not stirred up every time that the birds use it. According to seasonal rainfall, our pond varied from 55-60 sq. m (600-700 sq.ft) in area and the depth varied over the year from 1.2 - 1.5 metres (4 - 5 feet). It was partially emptied and cleaned once a year during the winter and took two to three days to refill. We avoided emptying it completely because it also had fish, plants and amphibians.

Many people had told us that it was not possible to have such a farm pond, warning us that the ducks in particular would eat all fish and frogs and destroy the plants. We proved them wrong! The ducks and geese were provided with an entry ramp on one side, and they tended to use this all the time, leaving other areas of the pond sides alone. The Marsh Marigolds, *Caltha palustris*, and Bogbean, *Menyanthes trifoliata,* thrived in these areas. (While they were becoming established, they were given wire-netting protection for a few months). In the deeper areas we even had a couple of Water Lilies, *Nymphaea alba*, while Canadian Pondweed, *Elodea canandensis*, increased the oxygen levels as well as providing food and shelter for smaller pond organisms. The fish were given safe havens by placing a few bricks covered with flagstones on the bottom

The most practical method of constructing a brand new pond is to dig a hole and line it with heavy-duty butyl rubber sheet, as referred to earlier. There are alternatives such as concrete or using a pre-formed plastic pond. The former needs a lot of heavy work and the latter is likely to be too small for your needs.

If you do plan to undertake the construction yourself, you can hire a machine that should dig a hole in a weekend. When you have made the pond to the right shape, with a shallow entrance ramp and with shallow shelves for marginal plants, you will need to go over the surface carefully and remove any protruding or sharp stones which could damage the lining once the pond has been filled. The hole is then lined with sand and the liner laid in place. The overlap around the edges should be weighted down with stones. A warm summer's day is the best time as the sun helps to make the liner more flexible. Gradually fill the pond and the liner will stretch and fill the space. When it is full, any surplus liner can be trimmed off, while flat stones around the edge over the remainder provide a neat edging.

There needs to be a shallow side or a ramp so that geese can walk in and out easily. They are adept at leaping into the water from a steep sided bank but need to be able to walk out again. Ours soon learnt to walk in and out the same way.

The edges of a well used pond can deteriorate into a muddy morass if the pond is insufficient for the number of geese, so ensure that that it is large enough both for the present flock and its possible expansion. It might be a good idea to have the capacity to fence off the pond from your geese from time to time so that it can

A pond made of heavy-duty butyl in the course of construction. (H.D. Sharman)

recover from their vigorous activities. Any depredations caused by drilling bills and muddy webs around the edges of the pond can also be mitigated by the use of *Nicospan*, a nylon mesh through which plants can grow.

It is important to remember that if water is extracted from an existing stream, or if it is dammed or diverted in any way, it is necessary to obtain permission from the *Environment Agency*. Where drains are used to cater for run-offs, it is important that it does not go onto a neighbour's land. The cleanliness of natural water courses is also protected by law, so it is essential that pollution does not happen.

To meet water regulations, an outside tap is required to have a valve inserted between it and a hose-pipe, so that there is no back-flow of water. Such valves are widely available in garden centres.

In winter the water supply can freeze. There are a number of ways of dealing with this. Standing water pipes can be lagged with insulation. It is also possible to bind purpose-made electrical tape around the water feed pipe, providing just enough heat to prevent freezing, but this does need access to a power supply. If you are carrying water to pour onto ice to assist its breakup, it should always be cold, not hot. This may seem to be against common sense, but it is a fact that ice is broken up more effectively by the application of cold water. Whatever you do, don't ever add anything to the water - not salt which is dangerous to all birds, nor as one hapless smallholder tried, anti-freeze - unless you want to poison all your geese!

Some of the author's geese enjoying fallen crab apples. These and other trees also provided shading and wind shelter for them. (Katie Thear)

The same geese in winter. Domestic geese are hardy and can cope with the cold, but water supplies must be assured. Ornamentals, such as Sheldgeese, need extra protection. (Katie Thear)

Feeding

A fair white goos wears feathers on hys back,
That gaggles still, much like a chattering pye.

(Pleasant Conceits, 1593. T. Churchyard)

It has already been mentioned several times, that good grass provides the basis of a goose's diet. But grass stops growing in winter, and the nutrient value declines considerably. At times such as these, or when there is a summer shortage of grazing, it is necessary to supplement the diet. Breeding birds also need supplements in order to ensure that deficiency diseases do not affect hatches, while young stock need a balanced ration in order to grow properly. Some people give their geese a little grain every day. We always did with ours, at the same time as we gave the ducks and chickens their afternoon grain ration.

It is important to remember that if you are changing the diet in any way, it should be done gradually as geese are conservative eaters and do not like sudden change.

Grain

Grain, particularly wheat, is the most common feed supplement. Different grains vary in their palatability and protein content. Wheat seems to be universally popular, but oats are often disliked, although they are particularly good in winter. Rolled barley or barley meal is suitable for fattening geese, but again, they may not be popular with the birds, and may need to be mixed in with other foods.

Bags of mixed grain are available, and the geese love this, in particular the maize content. The normal mix in proprietary bags is three-quarters wheat to one quarter kibbled or chopped maize. It is important to be aware however, that this can be too fattening for breeders. Particularly greedy birds may even pick out the yellow maize first! Domestic geese are hardy birds of the northern hemisphere, and if given too much supplementary food can become fat and lazy, with an obvious effect on breeding.

Some breeders prefer to give the grain ration in a little water, so that it is easier for the geese to eat. We never found this to be necessary with domestic geese, although it is appreciated by some ornamental breeds. However, young geese being introduced to grain for the first time may be encouraged to take it if it has been slightly softened by being in water.

As a general rule of thumb, provide just enough grain that the geese can clear up in fifteen minutes. Late afternoon is a good time to give a grain ration.

Grit and oystershell

It is essential that geese have access to clean, coarse sand or insoluble poultry grit all year round. It enables the gizzard to function properly, so that there is an adequate break-down of the grasses and other food material. The grit acts like small mill stones when the powerful muscles of the gizzard contract and relax during the digestive process.

Crushed oystershell is also beneficial because it ensures that there is an adequate balance of calcium and phosphorus, both needed for egg shell production. Geese will usually pick up what they need, if grit and oystershell are made available in a small container in a convenient place.

If you are using eggs in the kitchen, the shells can be washed, dried and crushed before being recycled into the grit ration. They will be readily accepted, but it is obviously important to ensure that they have been thoroughly cleaned, in order to avoid the risk of disease.

Proprietary feeds

Proprietary feeds are compound rations that have been formulated as a balanced meal for specific ages and requirements of waterfowl. They are available as crumbs, pellets or as loose meal in formulations such as the examples given below:

Waterfowl proprietary feeds	Protein	Oil	Fibre
Starter crumbs - goslings from hatch	19%	4.5%	4.5%
Grower pellets - young geese to finish	15%	3.25%	7%
Breeder pellets - breeding birds	16%	4.5%	6.5%

The starter crumbs are small and easily eaten by goslings. Grower pellets can, if necessary be used as a supplement to grass right through to slaughter weight. Breeder pellets are specially formulated for adult breeders so that the right balance of nutrients and minerals are available for breeding. Deficiencies can result in poor hatches and deformities in the goslings.

Drinking water

Ensure that there is always fresh water for geese to drink. For newly-hatched goslings, the container should have restricted apertures such as wire guards to prevent them jumping in and getting wet, fouling the water and becoming chilled. You can place the water container onto a mesh platform to prevent the litter becoming wet. Ensure that there is always sufficient clean water as goslings grow rapidly and consume copious amounts. For larger birds, a bucket placed in a rubber tyre is quick and easy to refill. On a larger scale, a low access field tank with automatic re-fill is the best option.

Some of the author's geese enjoying their wheat ration. Some breeders prefer to give grain in water so that it is more palatable, but we never found this to be the case. (Katie Thear)

Storing feeds

All feedstuffs should be protected from damp. Mouldy foods can introduce disease and have been known to kill waterfowl. Vermin also introduce disease and every effort should be made to exclude them.

Metal or plastic dustbins, preferably with a screw top are ideal, but remember that rats can gnaw their way through thick plastic, so if they are likely to be a problem, stick to metal containers.

Feeding goslings and growers

Geese grow fastest during the first four months, so their nutritional needs during this period need to be met fully if they are to grow a large frame and develop to their full potential. Skimping on feed costs during the early months is likely to be counter productive in the end, whether you are raising breeders or birds for the table. Geese fed properly during the first few months will mature more quickly and reproduce best. At the same time, growth should be gradual so it is important not to over-feed. Too much protein during the growing period can result in too rapid a growth rate, leading to slipped wing conditions. (See Health).

Goslings can be offered starter crumbs from day one, beginning with just a few placed on a non-slip surface. Replenish them regularly so that there is always enough for their needs, but be sure to clear away any unwanted feed. They include around 19-20% protein.

You should be able to obtain waterfowl starter crumbs which will ensure that there is also enough niacin content, as waterfowl need more than twice as much as chickens and it is essential for their development. If your stockist cannot supply them, chick crumbs can be used as an alternative. However, it is important to make sure that these chick crumbs do not contain coccidiostats as these are harmful to ducklings and goslings. Avoid giving dry mash to goslings, as not only will there be considerable wastage but young birds can choke and die.

The young goslings can also be offered some fresh grass. They can be turned out onto pasture as long as they are fully protected against predators, and from wind and rain. Goslings are voracious feeders so the covered run must be moved regularly to fresh grass. Ours always had their first trip out in a covered house and run that was placed into one end of the polytunnel greenhouse, so they were doubly protected.

After three weeks, the goslings can be given two feeds of starter crumbs a day, giving them just enough to clear up in 15 minutes. Once they are feeding throughout the day on good young grass, change to feeding them just once a day, in the evening. As they grow, their water and feed containers will need to be changed in order to ensure that all the birds can feed at the same time. Strong troughs that cannot be turned over are suitable. If they are only half filled each time, then wastage will be minimised. Provide insoluble grit at all times.

From four to eight weeks, grower pellets can be introduced instead of the starter crumbs. Any change in the diet should always be gradual. Grower pellets that are specially formulated for waterfowl are available. Depending on the supplier, these will have a protein level of 15-18%.

By eight weeks goslings should be getting much of their nutritional needs from the young green grass. Good pasture will have a protein content of about 16%. A high white clover content is also beneficial for young birds. Kitchen garden salad vegetables are also popular. The earlier they can go out on grass the better, but it needs to be fresh, new grass on land that has been fallow for a period, so that they are not at risk from parasites such as gizzard worm. If this cannot be guaranteed, it may be necessary to worm the stock on a regular basis. (See Health).

From 3 - 4 months you can either drop the daily feed altogether, change it to wheat only, or maintain the grower ration, depending on the quality of the grass.

By late summer the nutritional value of grass begins to decline, so supplementary feeding in the form of grower pellets or grain will be necessary again.

For details on fattening geese for Christmas, please see Table Geese.

Geese sharing pasture with cattle. They also cohabit well with sheep and horses. (Katie Thear)

Feeding breeders

Adult breeders will also obtain most of their nutritional needs from grass. This can be supplemented with wheat, where necessary. Richer foods are not necessary otherwise they may get too fat so that breeding performance is affected.

In winter, however, it is advisable to give them a proprietary waterfowl breeder's ration, rather than grain. As referred to earlier, this ensures that they are receiving the right balance of nutrients and minerals so that their progeny are not at risk of developing deficiency diseases. A breeder ration can be fed from November until the breeding period is over. Then, if necessary, they can go back to having wheat, although it must be emphasised again that grass should be the main constituent of their diet.

Geese make nesting areas quite readily, but often have a tendency to share nests. These are some of the author's nesting in a hedge, having ignored the houses made available for them.

This is a better behaved goose! She has decided that a garden shed is ideal for her purposes. Note the size of the nest!

A Chinese goose egg compared with a large size chicken egg. Embden and Toulouse eggs are even bigger, but they are fewer in number.
(Photos: Katie Thear)

Breeding

A wild goose never laid a tame egg. (Traditional saying)

A goose generally lays for about four months between February and June, although there are obviously some that lay for longer than this. The frequency of laying is around two eggs every three days. At the beginning of the laying period and with first layers, eggs may be laid in different places, even in the open field. These need to be gathered up promptly as they can be attacked as a source of food by hungry magpies or corvids. After this initial period the goose will settle into a routine of laying in the same place.

If the goose is required to hatch her own eggs, it will be advisable to provide a number of suitable nesting places which are quiet, with plenty of clean straw and which above all can be made safe against the invasion of vermin and predators during the nesting period. By the same token it also pays to be prepared to use an incubator in conjunction with sitting geese, and to have it up and running ready to use as soon as the laying period begins.

Eggs

Select only those eggs for incubation that are well shaped, smooth, large and without cracks. Always handle them gently and with clean hands. Incubating small eggs will produce correspondingly small goslings. Overlarge eggs may be double yolked and should be avoided. Eggs should also be clean. The odd bit of mud or straw can be removed with a small brush, but badly soiled eggs should be washed in clean warm water which includes an egg sanitant. Eggs that are to go into an incubator should always be washed in this way. Never wash eggs in cold or dirty water as this can lead to infection penetrating the pores of the shell.

Eggs laid at the beginning of the season, during the first couple of weeks, will not hatch as well as those laid later on. This may be due to a gradual reduction in the thickness of the eggshell. By the same token, those laid towards the end of the season, with thinner shells, are more likely to harbour infection.

Eggs that are for incubation should be kept for as short a period as possible, a week or ten days at the most. They should be in cool conditions, with a reasonably even temperature and away from daylight. A cellar is ideal, or a dark corner of a cool outhouse, but not in a refrigerator. Ideally they should be stored broad end upwards at an angle of about 40 degrees, and rotated once a day to prevent the contents sticking to the inner membrane. The air humidity in the UK is suitable for storing eggs in this way, but in drier climates and conditions some dampness may be advisable. Many breeders favour storing goose eggs on damp sand.

Structure of a goose egg

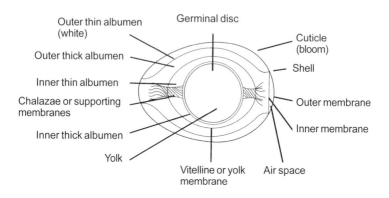

Outer thin albumen (white)

Outer thick albumen

Inner thin albumen

Chalazae or supporting membranes

Inner thick albumen

Yolk

Germinal disc

Cuticle (bloom)

Shell

Outer membrane

Inner membrane

Vitelline or yolk membrane

Air space

Egg broken open

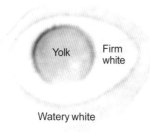

Yolk

Firm white

Watery white

Egg candling

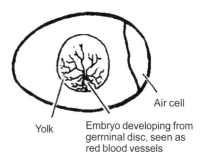

Air cell

Yolk

Embryo developing from germinal disc, seen as red blood vessels radiating outwards.

Size of air cell in relation to incubation time

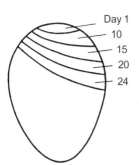

Day 1
10
15
20
24

This shows the size that the air cell should be at different stages of incubation, so that there is enough oxygen for the developing embryo.

If the air cell is too small, it indicates that the humidity is too high.

If the air cell is too large, it shows that too much water is being lost and the humidity is too low.

Natural incubation

Once the goose has chosen her nest, she will lay her eggs in it until she has a clutch, which could be between 8 -12 eggs. Once she begins to sit, she will stop laying and will be unlikely to commence again until the next season. However, if eggs are regularly removed from the nest, one by one, she may not notice and will go on laying for longer. Eggs collected can be incubated artificially or put under a broody hen, bantam or Muscovy duck.

Worm broody birds at the outset and check and dose for external parasites. The nest can also be dusted for mites. The protected nests that you have provided may be rejected by mother goose for a place under a hedge or even against a wall. If this happens, you can try to move the nest to a safe place but she may object and abandon it. The alternative is to build the protection around her. Here again it pays to be prepared, as a suitable coop and run can be made beforehand to place over the sitting bird. It will need to be big enough for her to get up and walk about. Although a goose will continue to sit in the open in almost any weather conditions, her goslings will be vulnerable to cold winds and rain and need good weather protection. During the day the pen can be open at one end so she can have contact with the gander. A goose will not eat a great deal whilst sitting, but food and water should be provided at a point where she will have to get up and walk to it. Wheat in the drinking water is entirely suitable. A shallow, heavy-based pan or bowl of water for bathing will also be appreciated, and will help her to keep clean and free from mites.

If two geese make nests nearby, it is advisable to erect a chicken wire wall between them, otherwise they may interfere with each other, trying to steal eggs and even finishing up on one nest, so that one clutch is abandoned. Two geese on the same nest never works properly as they seldom seem to be as dedicated as a sole sitter, and eggs can be left to go cold. A sitting goose may also abandon her eggs if she is young and inexperienced, or is badly disturbed by people or animals. If this happens, you can, if you are quick enough, transfer the eggs to the incubator. They should not be left for more than an hour.

After the first seven days of sitting, the eggs can be quietly borrowed from the nest, candled and returned until they are all checked. Candling is a process where a bright light is shone through the egg to view the developing embryo. A torch can be used, or a purpose-made candler bought from a specialist supplier.

At this time a properly developing embryo should look like a blob in the middle of the egg with red strands radiating outwards from it. If there is no sign of this, then the egg is clear and not fertile. If there is no air sac and there are dark blobs moving about inside the shell, the egg is rotten and should be discarded at once.

Surplus fertile eggs can be put under other broody birds if they are available. Hens and Muscovy ducks are good sitters and mothers, and can hatch goose eggs.

As a general guide, the number of eggs that can be placed under a broody is as follows:

Hen: 4-6 goose eggs
Muscovy duck: 5-7 eggs
Bantam: 2 eggs.

The number also depends on the size of the bird and that of the eggs. Eggs from a heavy breed like the Embden are larger than those laid by a Chinese goose.

Before putting eggs under a duck or hen, make certain that the bird is really broody. If she has settled, she will puff up her feathers and feel hot to the touch in the breast area. If necessary, she can be given some pot eggs to encourage broodiness. Once sitting tight, she is ready and the goose eggs can be introduced, one by one, while the dummy eggs are removed. Provide her with protected conditions such as a combined coop and run and include food, grit and water nearby.

During the incubation period a goose will turn her eggs during the day. This is essential for the developing embryo, and mother goose knows by instinct just what is required. Other smaller birds have the same instincts but may not be able to turn heavy goose eggs, so it is necessary to intervene and turn them gently and quietly at least twice a day. Each egg can be clearly marked with a cross and circle on opposite sides so a check can be made each time. Hens are not water birds, and will not bathe before returning to the nest. To mimic the effects of the waterfowl mother, sprinkle the eggs with warm water every day or two after the first week, until the 27th day. Do not be tempted to dunk the poor hen in a bucket of water as some have advocated, as this may put her off and the nest could be abandoned.

Goslings will start to hatch from around 28 days, but this can vary depending on the breed. It is a critical time, for a goose with her big feet may accidentally break the shell, particularly in late hatchings where the shell wall is thinner. Some goslings can be lost in this way. This risk can be reduced by transferring some eggs to an incubator at the final stage for hatching. The resulting goslings can then be slipped under her at night. This should work out, but if she does not accept them, remove them immediately and rear them separately. Observe carefully during this hatching period! After some goslings have hatched, the mother may walk off with them, forgetting the remaining eggs in the nest. If this occurs, transfer the remaining eggs immediately to the incubator.

Artificial incubation

An incubator is essential for anyone planning to hatch goslings on a regular basis. The machine will need to be in a stable environment away from strong temperature and humidity fluctuations. A spare bedroom or store room is ideal, but avoid cold, damp out-houses.

Goose eggs are large and need deeper than normal trays to accommodate them and the tall goslings when they hatch. (Curfew Incubators)

Purpose-made goose incubators are available. These have deeper shelves to cater for the large goose eggs and the tall goslings when they hatch. If you are using a general purpose incubator, remember to allow extra space. An incubator which is stated as having an egg capacity of 60 will normally be referring to hen eggs. The equivalent number of goose eggs would be 24.

A new incubator will need to meet all present and possible future needs. There are plenty to choose from, but the machine will need to accept goose eggs in sufficient numbers to be practical. The basic choice is between a table top model and a larger cabinet model. A modern electric incubator will have fan-assisted air circulation, accurate electronic controls and automatic or semi-automatic egg turning facilities. If you do need to incubate the eggs of other birds, there should be a facility for different internal trays to hatch the varying-sized eggs.

If the hatching enterprise grows, it may be more practical to add an additional machine than to begin with a very large one. It is useful to have a separate hatching area for the chicks or goslings to move about during their drying off period. If the enterprise merits it, a separate hatcher can be purchased, but a cabinet incubator with a separate hatching drawer may be the best option at the outset.

It is possible to buy small cheaper incubators without many automatic facilities, but they are not really suitable for incubating goose eggs on a regular basis. It is time-consuming having to turn the eggs manually several times a day. Turning is vital for the correct development of the embryo so that it does not become stuck to the internal membrane, and that waste products can be properly absorbed by the membrane and do not build up toxicity.

Clean and test the performance of the incubator, and leave it running for at least 24 hours before use. Before transferring the eggs from storage to the incubator, bring them into the incubator room overnight, to bring them gradually up to room temperature. In this way, there is less of a temperature change 'shock'. It is not a good idea to try and incubate waterfowl and chicken eggs at the same time for they hatch at different times and their humidity requirements also differ.

The incubator will need to provide a temperature of 37.5C at the heart of the egg during the incubation period, with a humidity level of 55%. A few days before hatching, at the 'pipping' stage when the goslings take up their position ready to break out of the shell, egg turning should cease. At this stage, the temperature is slightly reduced, to 37.0C, while the humidity is raised to 75%. This makes it easier for the goslings to crack and break out of the shell.

Candling after a week can show which eggs are developing properly. Those that are clear or showing signs of going bad must be eliminated from the incubation process. Candlers are available from incubator suppliers or you can make your own with a torch inside a box. Clear eggs cannot be eaten once they have been in the incubator, but they can be blown and washed out, and will be gladly accepted by egg decorating crafts people. Regular candling also shows whether the air cell inside the egg is developing properly. Its size relative to the days into incubation shows the humidity in relation to the air content. If it is too large, the humidity is too low. If too small, the humidity is too high and there is not enough oxygen for the embryo to survive. (See diagram on page 62).

Another method of assessing humidity is to weigh the egg at regular intervals to see whether it is losing weight at the correct rate. Weight loss needs to be at the rate of 11-13% from commencement of incubation to the 'no turning' stage.

Pipping begins with the goslings starting to break through the shell a day or

Geese are normally excellent at incubating, hatching and rearing their gosllings. (L.C. Allington)

two before hatching. It can take 2-3 days before the gosling is finally out so do not give up too soon. It is best to avoid 'helping' a gosling out unless it is quite clear that there is a difficulty. If this is the case, wipe the egg with a clean flannel that has been dipped in warm water. If nothing happens, extend the break in the shell slightly and extremely carefully, but stop immediately if bleeding occurs. Wipe the shell again and try later, but at this stage, you have done all you can.

If there is a separate hatching area, transfer the pipping eggs to that. As the goslings hatch, remove the discarded shells to make room for the others. Once the goslings have fluffed up and are active they can then be transferred to their brooding or rearing quarters.

A word of warning: do not let the first gosling see you before it has seen its compatriots, otherwise you will be imprinted as 'mother goose, and it will want to follow you everywhere in future!

Optimum conditions for the incubation of goose eggs

Egg storage (before incubation) Temperature: 15-18C Relative humidity: 75%
(Leave at normal room temperature for 24 hours before placing in the incubator).

Incubation (Day 1 to pipping) Temperature: 37.5C Relative humidity: 55%

Hatching (Pipping to emergence) Temperature: 37C Relative humidity: 75%

Depending on the breed, incubation from day 1 to hatch varies from 30 days for light breeds to 36 days for some heavy breeds. Pipping normally takes place 2-3 days before hatching.

Elements of rearing goslings

Suspended heat lamp

Stable feeder for starter crumbs

Walls to confine them to the heated area.

Placed in a vermin-proof environment

Drinker that they cannot climb into

A section of clean turf can be given to them to prevent them pulling at each other's feathers.

Outside rearing pen

The sooner the goslings go out, the better.

Night-time shelter with drop-down door

Clean, new grass that has not previously been used by poultry or waterfowl.

Confining fence. To provide regular access to new grass, this could be moveable. To provide protection from foxes, it could be electrified.

Dealing with splayed legs

The legs can be tied together with soft tape until they are straight again.

Learning to feed and drink

Hold it gently and dip the end of the bill into the feeder or drinker. Avoid getting water into the nostrils.

Goslings (and adult geese) are easy to drive from one pasture to another, or into a house.
(Early Bird Products)

Rearing goslings

Newly hatched goslings should not be removed from the incubator or hatcher until
they have dried out and fluffed up. If there are just a few, they can be placed in a
box in a warm place, such as by the side of an AGA, or even in a ventilated airing
cupboard for the first night. After that, they will need a more spacious brooder,
but if the rearing pen is in an outhouse with low night-time temperatures, it may
be best to keep them in the house for the first week. One of the most effective,
temporary brooders that I have used, is a large, semi-rigid, polypropylene weed-
ing bag of the sort widely available in garden centres. Placed in the conservatory
with a heating lamp suspended above it, it works well. Alternatively, a large card-
board box can be used. On a larger scale, a purpose-made brooding area in an
outbuilding is the norm.

Initially, use an old towel or piece of blanket on the floor so that the birds do
not slip and damage their legs or joints. Once they are active and eating, this can
be replaced with wood shavings. Before this, they may try and eat the shavings.

In the rearing pen, put a maximum of ten goslings together under a small lamp.
A larger 250 watt brooder lamp with a canopy will normally cater for 25 goslings.
Use a ceramic bulb in the lamp as it is reliable and less likely to fail than the other

type. If a lamp fails during the night, all the goslings could die. The heat lamp is suspended above the pen and raised from time to time as the birds grow. Newly hatched goslings under a lamp do not move very much so watch and see how they are. If they are panting, it is too hot and the lamp should be raised. Generally, the temperature at ground level should be 27C (80F) for the second week and 21C (70F) for the third week. The height of the lamp can also be regulated by the behaviour of the goslings. If they crowd to the centre of the space beneath the lamp, they are cold and the lamp should be lowered. If they fan out to the far edge of the pen away from the area below the lamp, they are too hot and the lamp should be raised.

The pen should provide protection from damp, cold, draughts and predators like rats or mink. Mice can also be a nuisance as they can contaminate the food, so they must be kept away. Goslings grow rapidly, so the floor area they require has to expand with them. They need up to a 900 sq. cm (1 sq. ft) per bird of floor space during the first week, double the amount in the second week and double the amount again for the next two weeks.

For the first 48 hours after hatching goslings do not need feeding as they have absorbed the yolk from the egg. However water can be provided immediately and waterfowl rearing pellets when they are 48 hours old. If waterfowl rations are not available, moistened chick crumbs (which do not include a coccidiostat) sprinkled with a little brewer's yeast are suitable. The brewer's yeast provides the vitamin B that they need. Goslings need to eat greens as soon as possible so a small turf or shredded dandelion leaves can also be offered straight away. This also helps to prevent the goslings pulling at other's feathers, particularly if these have become wet and spiky. It should not be possible for them to climb into the drinkers for the same reason. Place food and drink in the coolest part of the pen.

Keep a regular eye on the goslings and talk to them softly so that they are not frightened. The confidence they gain from sensitive handling will pay dividends later as they are less likely to be alarmed when approached. As the goslings begin to grow, chopped barley straw or wood shavings can be put down as litter. Provide them with insoluble grit in a small container. They will take this as needed.

After a couple of weeks, the goslings can be put out into a protected coop and run during warm sunny days. They are still vulnerable to cold and rain so place plenty of straw in the coop and make sure that they know that it is there. Ensure that the coop and run are safe against rats and other dangers. If it should rain or the temperature drops quickly, cover the pen straight away. Goslings will attack the grass underfoot with relish, so they should be on ground that has not been grazed by adult geese as they can pick up gizzard worm. Fine young spring grass will be ideal, but keep an eye on them as the coop may have to be moved onto fresh grass during the day.

At three weeks the goslings can be out every day, but will still need protection from bad weather and predators, and kept away from other livestock. The exercise will help them to grow strong legs to carry their rapidly increasing bodyweight. At this stage, they will appreciate a shallow bowl of water to get their feet and heads wet. This keeps them healthy and stimulates preening. They should not be immersed in water, however, until their backs are fully feathered at around 6 weeks old. Between 3 and 4 weeks introduce more grower's pellets into the ration each day so that from the fourth week they are wholly on the them. Again, the ideal is for waterfowl grower pellets. At this stage a little wheat can also be added to the diet, and the insoluble grit will enable them to break it down in the gizzard. This is the time when quills are growing strongly, and if their weight cannot be supported, the wing will drop. (See page 90 and follow the procedures outlined). If the condition does occur, it probably means that there is too much protein in the diet, so immediate steps can be taken to reduce it. Further details of feeding are in the Feeding chapter.

Sexing

It is useful to be able to determine the sex of goslings, but it is difficult to do so when they are very young.

Auto-sexing

This is where the down colour of the males and females is different. The only pure breeds that are auto-sexing are Pilgrim, West of England and Shetland geese, where there is a colour difference in the goslings. Females are greyer than the males. In some strains the colour difference is not clear so check for lighter or darker bill and webs. Some strains of Embden and Sebastopol goslings can also be sexed by down colour as the males are lighter than the females.

Vent sexing

This should not be attempted without having first had the technique demonstrated by someone experienced, for it is easy to damage the gosling. Hold the gosling gently, head downwards, so that the vent is between the thumb and forefinger. Gently press the second finger which is behind the bird's back, and at the same time, push the forefinger back slightly so that the vent is exposed. Now, with the other hand, hold the vent on each side with the thumb and forefinger and press down slightly in order to open the vent. In the male, the penis will be seen as a tiny pink projectile. It will be necessary to check several goslings before the distinction is clear, but once achieved, sexing becomes a relatively easy technique. Vent sexing can also be carried out on larger birds, in which instance it will be necessary to have someone else to assist.

Sexual characteristics

As goslings grow, their sexual characteristics become more distinct. African and Chinese males are much larger than females and have a larger knob at three to four months. Generally, ganders grow taller and larger than geese, with longer, thicker necks. Their calls are shriller and more high pitched. The head is often longer and flatter than that of the female, but this does vary with individual breeds.

As a goose comes into lay, the line of the lower body often drops. Ganders are more aggressive and hiss more, particularly when the breeding season commences. At this stage, it will be obvious which is the male and which is the female. Once geese have been sexed, leg rings can be used to identify them. Leg rings are available in different sizes from the *British Waterfowl Association.* (See page 81).

As far as mating is concerned, the larger, heavier breeds normally will have a higher rate of fertility if they have access to swimming water at least 40cm (16in) deep. Both sexes dip their heads in the water together, then the goose will spread herself out and the gander will mount her to mate, holding on to her neck for balance. He lets out a great cry as he slips off.

If no pond is available, mating will take place in the same way on land, but the sexes still need water to dip their heads into. If the mating has been successful, eggs will become fertile 3-4 days afterwards and remain so for a couple of weeks.

Comparison of vents of goslings

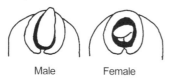

Male   Female

Do not attempt this without having had the technique demonstrated, for it is easy to damage the goslings.

Comparison of heads

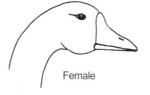

Female

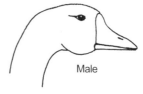

Male

Comparison of abdomen line

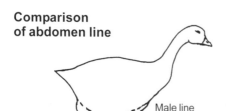

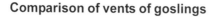

Male line

Female line

The line of the abdomen and paunch is lower in a female approaching lay.

The head of the female is more rounded and finer than that of the gander.

Bear in mind that individual breeds vary, so these differences may not be easily apparent, eg, the head of the Roman breed is more rounded anyway, while the males of some breeds have distinct paunches.

Table geese

A goose is a poor thing, too much for one, not enough for two. (Attributed to Queen Elizabeth 1).

Queen Elizabeth 1 was not complimentary about the culinary qualities of geese, as the quotation above indicates, but it should be remembered that this was in the days before heavy breeds had been developed as table birds in Britain. Mrs Beeton was far more enthusiastic, stating that:
"A large goose for 5s 6d is sufficient for eight or nine persons."

Cramming a goose in order to make its liver swollen for paté production is thankfully illegal in Britain, but not in other European countries.

Michaelmas geese

If you are raising geese for meat they can be ready in October. This is the Michaelmas or green goose. It will not be as plump as the fattened Christmas goose but still makes a very tender roast dinner. It will be less fatty than a fattened goose, which may be more desirable. If you want leaner meat, Chinese or African geese produce a leaner carcase than Embdens or Toulouse. A relatively lean goose is one that has foraged for most of its diet and had just enough supplementary grain or pellets to keep it growing and well fleshed out. Geese can also be killed in October and frozen for Christmas. They will be smaller and leaner, but you will save the time and expense of fattening them. However, most customers are look- ing for plump, fresh geese that are at their maximum weight at Christmas.

Heavy breeds, if they have been fed regularly on concentrates, can be killed at 8 - 10 weeks. They can weigh up to 4.5kg (10 lb). To maximise growth at this age, you need to reduce their amount of exercise and bring them inside overnight. They are ready as soon as they are fully feathered. Beyond 12 weeks, food conversion declines as they grow much more slowly and they can moult which makes for lots of pin feathers. This can make plucking a nightmare.

If you continue to feed grower or finisher rations during the summer period when there is plenty of good grass, you are incurring extra expense and your geese will finish early, perhaps as early as 13-14 weeks. This is a bad time for plucking so it is better to feed less concentrates at this time. If you use the pasture fully and restrict or stop supplementary feeding altogether, the geese will not grow as rap- idly during this period, but this will not have any effect on future growth.

Christmas geese

If the geese are to be run on for the Christmas market, they will need to be finished or fattened for three or four weeks to bring them up to maximum weight and plump condition. Do not continue to fatten longer than this as the birds will not continue to grow and you will be wasting time and money. The carcase should finish at three quarters of the live weight

Fattening geese need quiet, unstressful conditions. Handle them quietly and slowly and avoid any sudden changes in their diet or lifestyle. Ideally, they can be left on well drained pasture during the day but with restricted space so they do not use up too much energy. The use of moveable electric fencing may be appropriate.

Be sure to provide protection from wind and rain. If the ground becomes fouled or waterlogged move them onto fresh ground straight away. If there is no fresh grass available at this time, the geese can be kept in a concrete yard, although this is not an ideal situation. At night move them into their house slowly and quietly. The yard can then be brushed and hosed down so that it is clean for the geese the next day. Again, protection from adverse weather conditions is necessary. Geese are sociable birds so keep the flock together. If you remove some birds early, the rest may go off their food for a day or two.

All breeds will fatten up except Chinese. The heavy breeds and strains will fatten best of all. There are less pin feathers between 22 - 26 weeks so you should aim to kill and pluck the birds during this period, if possible, when they are in full feather. You can check whether they are fully feathered again after the moult as the primary feathers should reach back to the tail. The plumage should look smooth and solid with no downy feathers showing. All fattened geese should be killed by 10 months at the latest as they begin to go tough after that. Geese can be finished with proprietary waterfowl finisher pellets or they can continue on grower pellets. This is straightforward and time saving, but it is expensive. You can reduce the cost by feeding barley meal mixed with rolled barley. Alternatively, use a combination of cooked potatoes, finely chopped vegetables and spare milk, either skimmed or whole if you have it, mixed to a crumb consistency with barley or maize meal. Most of these foods will provide the high protein diet that the fatteners need. You can also feed mixed grains but not exclusively as their protein level is not high. If you do vary the diet, do so gradually so that the geese are not put off their food.

Killing and plucking

Whether you are slaughtering geese for your own consumption or for resale, you are obliged to do so humanely. Birds for slaughter come under the auspices of the Welfare of Animals (Slaughter or Killing) Regulations 1995 which require the birds to be electrically stunned before slaughter.

Killing The geese should not be fed for 12 hours before slaughter, but should have access to fresh water. The recommended method is to stun the bird first with an electrical stunner, then a sharp knife is inserted into the mouth and pushed up towards the eyes. It is then twisted sideways to sever the jugular vein. The bird should be suspended immediately to allow the blood to run to the head.

Plucking Remove the large feathers, then the small feathers and lastly the down. This can be done by hand or by using a plucking machine. Alternatively, the goose can be scalded beforehand by dipping for a couple of minutes in hot water at 65C (150F). The temperature and timing are important if the scalding is to be effective. Once scalded, the feathers and down should come out easily. When plucking, use short sharp strokes along the direction of feather growth, taking care not to tear the skin. If keeping the down and feathers, they need to be kept clean, so a bag tied over the top of the neck to prevent blood escaping will be necessary. If the bird has been dry plucked, hang it in a cold, dry airy place for several days.

Eviscerating First remove the head, feet and preen gland above the tail. Now make an incision between the vent and the breast bone. Insert a hand and loosen the organs from the body wall. Cut along the length of the neck and pull out the windpipe and oesophagus. Cut carefully around the vent to disconnect the intestines, then pull them all out. Now wash out the carcase with cold water. Remove the heart, gizzard and liver from the innards which can then be discarded. Cut around the edge of the gizzard then open it up to remove the inner bag with the grit and wash out. Cut the gall bladder away from the liver without puncturing it otherwise it will taint the meat.

Goose products

There are a range of products associated with geese, and these can provide an addition to the income that would normally be associated with table geese.

Feathers There is a market for goose feathers for anyone raising and plucking geese on a large enough scale. A large goose can yield up to 0.23kg (½ lb) of feathers. Unfortunately, imports of duck and goose down have reduced the price offered by merchants for goose feathers, and it is now less than £1 per lb.

If you are plucking sufficient geese and wish to make use of the feathers for home use, take care to keep the feathers clean. Sterilize them by placing them in a cotton bag and heating them in a low-medium oven for half an hour. The feathers and down can now be used for pillows. Use herringbone ticking which is featherproof, and double stitch the seams so that feathers don't come out. A pillow needs a combination of down and feathers if it is to maintain its shape. Opinion varies, but the proportion of feathers to down needs to be from 25 - 50%.

These days there is no longer a market for quills, but with a suitable feather a quill pen can be made at home. Who knows, it may also be an item that visitors to a waterfowl collection would consider buying as a novelty?

How to make a quill pen

With acknowledgments to J. Fitzgerald who wrote this article for *Practical Self Sufficiency* magazine, Issue No. 12, in September 1977.

①

Outer membrane

Underside of quill

First cut

Materials needed
Goose flight feather.
Sharp *Stanley* or craft knife.
Pair of sharp scissors.
Piece of thin metal (shim).
Shallow tin.
Silver sand.

②
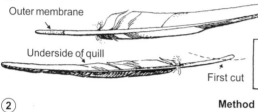

Internal membrane

Shoulder

Cut

Flange

③

④ Tines

Cut

Cut

Cut back

Cut

⑤

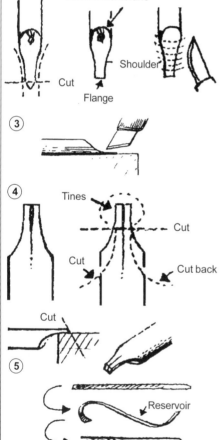

Reservoir

Method

1. Scrape off the transparent outer membrane covering the lower part of the quill with the thumb nail. It comes off easily.
Holding the feather with the underside uppermost, slice off the end of the quill in a long, diagonal cut, entering the blade about 2.5cm (1in) up the quill.

2. Trim the shoulders on each side to give a long flange, and then cut off the point with the scissors, making a square end.
Pull out the internal membrane which lies loosely in the barrel of the quill.
Using a lateral movement of the knife blade, scrape the inside of the barrel to give the ink a surface it can adhere to.

3. Lay the nib end of the quill, hollow side uppermost, flat down on a hard surface, and press down the blade hard, about 5mm (¼ in) along the nib flange, making a slit in it.

4. With the finger and thumb, squeeze the quill hard on either side of the slit, which will then run further up the quill like a ladder in a stocking.
Holding the end of the quill up to the light, notice how the entry of the blade has forced the tines apart so that there is a gap between them. This will have to be cut off up to the point where the tines lie flush together.

5. The nib can now be given its writing edge after it has been trimmed on either side to give the desired width. Lay it flat down, top uppermost, on the edge of a hard surface, and cut down firmly at a slant, giving a chisel-shaped end.
A metal reservoir can be made from thin metal foil (shim) cut into a strip approximately 5cm (2in) long and just wide enough to fit in the quill barrel.
To harden the quill, fill a shallow tin with silver sand and heat until too hot to touch. Remove from the heat and push the nib end into the hot sand until cooled.

Eggs People will buy fresh goose eggs at the farm gate or in the local market. However, unusual products do not sell themselves, so be prepared to encourage buyers, by highlighting the qualities of goose eggs and their uses, eg, they make great souffles or egg custard. A sheet of recipes is inexpensive to produce and can be given away with each egg purchase.

Clear eggs recovered from the incubator cannot be eaten, but they can be blown and sold to egg decorators in the craft market. To blow a goose egg, make a hole at the broad end of the egg and a smaller hole at the pointed end. Break up the contents by inserting and wiggling a skewer or similar implement, then blow the contents out. When emptied, wash the egg inside and out with clean water with some added bleach.

Goose Fat Goose fat which is soft, and pale yellow, has excellent qualities for cooking. It has a relatively low proportion of saturated fat - less than butter, lard, beef or pork - and a consequently higher proportion of mono-unsaturated fat and essential fatty acids.

The fat can be recovered first during evisceration and secondly when the goose is cooked. It will keep for 4-6 months in a sealed container in the refrigerator, or for a year in the freezer. Popular with cooks who are aware of its properties, goose fat can also be sealed into jars for resale. In recent years it has become recognised as a gourmet product.

Goose fat can be used for cooking potatoes, meats, pasta and vegetables. Roast potatoes are particularly delicious when cooked in this way.

Examples of commercial enterprises

Bulows Hatchery in Denmark have bred the large white Legarth goose. This has been exported worldwide and today provides the foundation for many of the commercial goslings available from British breeders. Britain's largest breeder is John Adlard of *Norfolk Geese* who now raises all his goslings from his own breeding stock. As well as selling geese, he supplies blown eggs to the egg-craft market.

Judy Goodman is a successful goose farmer, raising 3000 white Legarth Cross geese in Worcestershire each year, running them at around 100 birds per acre through the summer months. The geese have a supplementary feed of a wheat and barley mix, enriched with vitamins and minerals. They are slaughtered at 22-28 weeks, dry plucked and hung for 10 days. They are then cold eviscerated and sold oven-ready at weights from 4.5-6kg (10-13lbs).

Ann Botterill on the other side of the country, buys in around 1000 Legarth Cross goslings and raises them on pasture from May onwards. Their diet is supplemented with her farm grown wheat and oats. The geese are killed at 18-26 weeks, hung for 10 days and sold from Michaelmas onwards as long legged (plucked undrawn), weighing 5.5-8kg (12-18lbs) or oven ready at 4.5-6.5kg (10-14lbs).

Showing

Goosy, goosy gander, whither shalt thou wander? (Nursery rhyme)

Showing poultry can be an interesting and rewarding hobby, and is a good way of learning about what goes into making a good example of a particular breed. It is a good idea to visit shows where birds are being shown. Breeders are often helpful to a novice and much useful information can be obtained.

Waterfowl are shown at the agricultural shows during the spring, summer and autumn, and the specialised poultry shows during the winter months. Perhaps the most important shows for seeing geese are the *British Waterfowl Association* and *Devon and Cornwall Waterfowl Shows* which are both held in November. The *National Poultry Show* is held during the first weekend of December, while the *Federation Poultry Show* usually follows a fortnight later.

One of the first impressions that a newcomer has, is how big the geese can be at a national show. This is for a variety of reasons: it may be the first time that the visitor has seen geese close up, but it is also the case that exhibition strains are bigger than utility strains. At a premier show, it is also the case that only the very best birds are on display.

Show preparations

Before entering for any show it is a good idea to join a local poultry club or breed society first, and then to buy a copy of the *British Waterfowl Standards* or the *British Poultry Standards*. With geese, only the standardised domestic breeds are shown. The Standards show the best points for each breed, providing an ideal against which to measure examples of the respective breeds.

When showing for the first time, it is best to start with a local agricultural or poultry show, before contemplating any of the major shows. There is a lot to be learned by taking part, from the judges and from other breeders. The fees and rewards involved are modest, so it is a hobby that can be undertaken by anyone, whatever their means. However, if you do well at shows this can enhance the value of your stock. If you really want to do well, begin by purchasing good quality stock in the first place - they cost no more to keep than poor stock.

A show schedule, together with a form to fill in for entries, can be obtained from the relevant poultry show secretary. If you are unsure of anything, check with the secretary before returning the form, to avoid making a mistake.

Geese are shown in large pens and need to be able to stay in them for up to three days without being distressed. It is therefore a good idea to set up something

"Ready for the show, behaving nicely and showing myself to the best advantage. Where's the judge?" (Katie Thear)

similar at home beforehand, to accustom the birds to these conditions. Try to ensure that there are other geese nearby so as to replicate the show situation as much as possible and to minimise stress.

A day or two before travelling to the show, ensure that the geese are clean, particularly underneath, and clean up the legs and webs using a soft nailbrush and warm soapy water. Check also that the eyes and nostrils are clear. Having prepared the birds, keep them on clean litter before they leave.

Picking a winner from the flock comes with experience. A good breeder can spot a likely winner by two months old. Size is particularly important with geese and an undersized bird in its breed category is not likely to get far. Both size and condition can be maximised by proper feeding and good management throughout.

Breeders use a range of well-ventilated travelling boxes for their poultry, many of which are home made. The essential point is to provide cool, comfortable accommodation for the birds, in order to minimise any discomfort or stress on the journey to and from the show. The container should be secured so that it does not move in transit. If the journey is a long one you may have to stop en route to give the geese food and water. On arrival, collect the details from the secretary and transfer your birds to their allocated pens. Good luck!

Ornamental breeds

A late spring light to dance the wild goose chase (Traditional rhyme)

If you have extensive areas of water, you may be visited by migratory geese and other wildfowl for which you are not legally responsible. They come and go as they please, often spending the winter in Britain and then returning to Scandinavia and other areas of northern Europe. The situation with breeds that are not normally found in Britain is different. They will need to be kept in such a way that they do not escape into the wild. This means having to pinion them so that their ability to fly is restricted, or alternatively keeping them in aviary enclosures.

The sheldgeese of South America are less hardy than true geese of the Northern hemisphere so they will need protected or aviary conditions. Frost-bite can be very damaging to their feet.

Some breeds are easier to keep than others, so it is advisable for beginners to confine themselves to the more common species until they are more experienced. Three breeds that the BWA recommends for beginners are the Barnacle, the Pink-Footed and the White-Fronted goose. Bear in mind that some of the sheldgeese can be aggressive to other species so are best kept on their own. Some geese are rare, and keeping examples of them places a special responsibility on the owner.

Abyssinian Blue-Winged goose, *Cyanochen cyanopterus*
Originating in the mountains of Abyssinia, this medium-sized breed is grey brown with blue-grey shoulders and a green wing bar. It is quite hardy but can be quarrelsome. It is also fairly difficult to breed. The incubation period is 30-32 days.

Andean goose, *Chloephaga melanoptera*
The South American Andean goose has a reputation for being aggressive to other waterfowl, so is best kept separately. It has an upright stance and a slightly hooked, pink and black bill. The plumage is white with black wings and tail. It is fairly easy to breed, needing an incubation period of 30 days.

Ashy-Headed goose, *Chloephaga poliocephala*
A South American sheldgoose, this has an attractive soft grey head and neck (hence the name), with a reddish-brown breast and upper back. The flanks are barred in white and black. The bill is black while the legs and webs are orange and black. It needs protected conditions in winter and although it will breed in captivity, it can be aggressive to other waterfowl. The incubation period is 30 days.

Bar-Headed goose, *Anser indicus*
Aptly named, this goose has a white head with distinctive black bars across the top. The plumage is pale brown with a white stripe running along the side of the

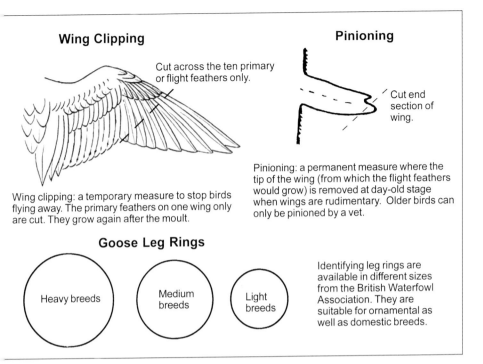

Wing Clipping

Cut across the ten primary or flight feathers only.

Wing clipping: a temporary measure to stop birds flying away. The primary feathers on one wing only are cut. They grow again after the moult.

Pinioning

Cut end section of wing.

Pinioning: a permanent measure where the tip of the wing (from which the flight feathers would grow) is removed at day-old stage when wings are rudimentary. Older birds can only be pinioned by a vet.

Goose Leg Rings

Heavy breeds

Medium breeds

Light breeds

Identifying leg rings are available in different sizes from the British Waterfowl Association. They are suitable for ornamental as well as domestic breeds.

neck. The bill and legs are orange. It breeds fairly readily in captivity, with an average incubation period of 27 days.

Barnacle goose, *Branta leucopsis*
This is a small, easily tamed goose which is a winter visitor to Britain from Scandinavia and Greenland. It has attractive black, grey and white plumage, with a black breast, crown and neck, and a distinctive white face. It is frequently found in waterfowl collections and breeds freely, with an incubation time of 24 days.

Bean goose, *Anser fabalis*
Breeding in northern Russia and Lapland, the Bean goose is a winter visitor to Europe, with a few occasionally arriving in Britain. Its name is related to the fact that it is traditionally partial to field crops of beans! Similar to, but slightly larger than the Greylag, it is brownish in colour with a dark brown head and neck, and an orange and black bill. The legs are orange. It has a distinctive 'kayak' call and is fairly easy to tame, although it does not nest readily in confinement. If it can be persuaded to do so, the incubation period is 28 days.

Brent goose, *Branta bernicla*
A small, dark-plumaged goose that overwinters in Britain, this has two races; a dark-bellied and a light-bellied. The former is from the European Arctic, while the latter breeds in the American Arctic. They are difficult to breed in captivity.

Canada goose, *Branta canadensis*

There are several sub-species of Canada geese which, as the name suggests, originate in Canada and Northern USA. It has been introduced to Europe and is now resident here. The Atlantic Canada, *Branta canadensis canadensis*, is the largest of the wild goose species. It has a large, brown body with a long black neck. The head is also black but it has white cheeks.

In the USA, the Eastern or Common Canada goose was admitted to the *USA Standard of Perfection* in the nineteenth century, and is classified as a light breed. It needs plenty of water so is only applicable to those who can supply this. It breeds readily in captivity, particularly if an island site is available, and has an average incubation time of 27 days.

Cereopsis goose, *Cereopsis novaehollandiae*

Also called the Cape Barren goose, this is from Australia so when kept in confinement here, it breeds in winter. The incubation period is 35 days. It is pale grey with black stippling and has a greenish bill and pinkish legs. Although it can become quite tame, it can be aggressive to other birds. Winter protection is vital.

Egyptian goose, *Alopochen aegyptiacus*

Although originating in Africa, this is quite hardy and is popular in collections because of its attractive plumage. It is buff and chestnut with green and black wings, while the bill and feet are pink. They are relatively easy to breed in captivity but can be aggressive to other birds. Incubation takes 30 days. The *American Standard of Perfection* has recognised the Egyptian as a light breed since 1874.

Emperor goose, *Anser canagicus*

The grand name suggests a large goose, but it is in fact, fairly small. It comes from Alaska and is silver-grey with black and white barring, while the head and neck are white with a black throat. The bill is bluish-pink and the legs are yellow. It is fairly quiet, easily tamed and will breed in captivity. For this, natural ground cover is required. The average incubation period is 24 days.

Greylag goose, *Anser anser*

As referred to earlier, this is the ancestor of most of the domestic breeds, apart from the Chinese. The name is thought to be from an old English word 'lag' meaning a line or edge, possibly referring to the edge of the wing which is pale, in contrast to the rest of the wing. Found all over Europe, it breeds in Britain, in the wild and in captivity. The incubation period is 28 days.

There are two races, the Western Greylag, *Anser anser anser*, and the Eastern Greylag, *Anser anser rubirostris*. They both have uniform grey plumage, but the Eastern is slightly paler and has a pinkish bill and legs, while those of the Western are orange. It is easy to see, therefore, why some of our domestic breeds have pink bills and legs while others are orange.

Canada geese preening by the lake side. (Clipart Collection)

Kelp goose, *Chloephaga hybrida hybrida*

Kelp geese are sheldgeese from South America and the Falklands, and are rarely bred in captivity. They graze on coastal plants, notably the Sea cabbage, and are obviously difficult to cater for in captivity. This is for the specialist only.

Magellan goose, *Chloephaga picta*

Also called the Upland goose, this is a big bird with white and grey plumage and dark barring. It is fairly easy to breed, requiring 30 days incubation, and is hardy.

Magpie goose, *Anseranas semipalmata*

In a class of its own, the Magpie goose of Australia has incomplete webbing on its feet because it is a tree climber. It requires protected, large aviary conditions, with a nesting platform, but is difficult to breed in captivity. This is for the specialist.

Ne-Ne goose, *Branta sandvicensis*

Also called the Hawaiian goose, the name Ne-Ne is an onomatopoeic representation of its call. It is fairly common in waterfowl collections, and it has been brought back from near extinction in the wild. An attractive, medium sized goose, its plumage is brown, black and light buff. It is reasonably hardy and is not difficult to breed in captivity. The incubation period is 29 days.

Orinoco goose, *Neochen jubata*

Another of the sheldgeese of South America, the Orinoco is not winter hardy and needs a large aviary. Difficult to breed in captivity, it is best left to specialists.

Pink-Footed goose, *Anser brachyrhynchus*
The Pink-Footed goose is smaller than the Greylag and is a fairly regular winter visitor to Britain. As the name suggests, the legs and webs are pinkish in colour, while the body is greyish-brown with a darker brown head and neck. The bill is relatively small and is black with a pinkish band. It adapts well to confinement and will nest quite freely in these conditions. Incubation is 27 days.

Red-Breasted goose, *Branta ruficollis*
This is my favourite amongst the ornamentals, with its beautiful black, white and chestnut red plumage, with black bill and legs. It is small in size and adapts well to captivity. It can sometimes be difficult to breed, but given the right, natural cover, it is more likely to be successful. Incubation takes 24 days.

Ruddy-Headed goose, *Chloephaga rubidiceps*
Another South American Sheldgoose, this is smaller than the Ashy-Headed. It has a reddish-brown head and neck with a white neck ring. The breast is orange-brown with black barrings, while the legs are orange and black. The bill is black. It will breed in captivity, but as with many of the Sheldgeese, it can be rather quarrelsome. It needs winter shelter.

Snow goose, *Anser sp.*
There are three types: the Lesser Snow goose, *Anser caerulescens hyperboreus,* the Greater Snow goose, *Anser caerulescens atlanticus*, and Ross's goose, *Anser rossii*. All are hardy and will cohabit well with other breeds in a collection. Ross's goose is the smallest and will breed well in captivity. Its incubation period is 22 days, while that of the Lesser and the Greater are 23 and 24 days, respectively.

Spur-Winged goose, *Plectopterus gambiensis*
This is a perching goose, adapted for climbing, so confinement can present a challenge. Unless it is pinioned, it will need to be kept in an aviary run with overhead netting. Difficult to breed in captivity, it is best left to the specialist.

Swan goose, *Anser cygnoides*
As referred to earlier, this is the ancestor of the Chinese goose and resembles the Brown Chinese variety, although its bill is longer and does not have a knob. It winters in China, although its breeding grounds are in Siberia. It needs sheltered conditions. It breeds fairly readily in captivity. Incubation takes 28 days.

White-Fronted goose, *Anser albifrons*
There are two races of the White-Fronted: the Siberian and Greenland. Both are brown with a black-barred breast and white forehead, but the former has a pink bill, while the latter's is orange. The Greenland also has slightly darker plumage. Easily tamed, the White-Front is often seen in waterfowl collections and will breed in captivity. It has a characteristic musical 'chuckle' call, so that it is often called the 'laughing' goose. There is also a Lesser White-Fronted goose, *Anser erythropus*, which is small in size and also breeds well in captivity. Incubation takes 25 days.

Health

Prithee pale-faced loon, where gottest thou that goose look?
(Shakespeare - Macbeth)

Geese are essentially very healthy birds and not subject to nearly as many ailments as other poultry. Where illness does occur, it is often the result of poor management, but if they are well looked after there should be few problems.

Preventing disease

Prevention through good husbandry is the key to avoiding problems. The main points to bear in mind are as follows:

• Buy healthy stock in the first place.
• Worm new stock and quarantine for 10 days before letting them join the others.
• Ideally, keep different ages separate - not always possible on a small scale.
• Provide housing that is dry, clean, windproof but well ventilated.
• Provide and replenish clean, dry floor and nest litter regularly.
• If swimming water is available, change it frequently.
• Ideally, feed proprietary pellets and grain only, and avoid anything mouldy.
• Provide fresh drinking water every day.
• Clean feeders and drinkers regularly.
• Take measures to get rid of rats that carry disease.
• Provide protection from predators.
• Avoid overstocking and provide plenty of room, both indoors and outside.
• Rotate grassland on a regular basis.
• Always put young goslings on fresh grass previously unused by other birds.
• Get to know your geese and watch for unusual behaviour.

Disease indicators

Checking the geese every day is essential if potential problems are to be spotted. It is amazing how quickly one gets to know the patterns of behaviour of individual geese just by spending time observing them. They are such interesting birds that this is hardly a chore, it seems to me.

The sooner an out-of-the-ordinary pattern of behaviour is detected, the more likely it is to detect a problem and put it right before it gets serious. Suspicious signs to look out for include the following:

• Eye, nasal or vent discharge.
• Lack of coordination.
• Limping or other unusual walk or stance.
• Loss of condition - dull feathers and eyes.
• Lethargy and sitting for long periods.
• Lack of, or excessive, appetite.
• Excessive thirst.
• Thinness, loss of weight.

Dealing with a problem

Despite everything, problems can still arise in well managed flocks. If a goose does display unusual symptoms, isolate it from the rest of the flock in case it is harbouring something infectious. A temporary pen with a shelter on one side, or a corner of a barn fenced off is suitable, as long as there is plenty of ventilation, while at the same time, avoiding draughts.

Give it fresh water and dry proprietary pellets and the chances are that it will recover. A little cider vinegar in the water may be beneficial. Plain, live yoghurt has probiotic features, and is also useful after an antibiotic course, to help reinstate the normal gut organisms. If there is no discernible improvement after a couple of days, or if the bird is getting worse, it needs veterinary attention.

If a condition is affecting several birds, seek veterinary advice immediately.

A-Z of problems

The following is a list of conditions that can affect geese, but it should be emphasised that most of them will probably never be encountered. They are included, however, because 'fore-warned is fore-armed', as long as the reader also bears in mind the other old adage, 'a little knowledge is a dangerous thing'. In between these two concepts, there is a sensible balance.

Aflatoxin Poisoning

Aflatoxins are produced by the moulds *Aspergillus flavus* and *A. parasiticus*. These are found on cereals, bread and other foodstuffs that are old or have not been stored properly. Never feed mouldy bread or old feeds to waterfowl!

Aspergillosis (Fungal pneumonia)

Aspergillus fumigatus fungus is the cause of this. It is found in mouldy hay, litter or feed. When the spores are inhaled, the fungus grows in the lungs. Goslings are particularly at risk It can be caused through poor hatchery and brooder conditions, hence the common name 'brooder pneumonia'. People can also be affected, a condition known as 'farmer's lung'. Symptoms are gasping and rapid breathing. Treatments are available but expensive. Prevention is best.

Botulism (Limber neck)

This condition is caused by toxins arising from the bacterium *Clostridium botulinum*. Stagnant water, perhaps with dead animals in it, is the usual cause, which is why all waterfowl need clean, well-oxygenated water when bathing. Symptoms include weakness, lack of coordination, and drooping of the wings, eyelids and neck, leading eventually to paralysis and death. An antitoxin is available but is only effective in mild cases. Prevention is best.

A listless goose sitting for long periods should be checked in case there is a problem. (Katie Thear)

Coccidiosis

This is unusual in geese, but can affect young goslings. Coccidia are organisms that affect the intestines and are passed in the droppings. The symptoms are severe: blood-stained, white diarrhoea, a hunched up stance and inability to stand properly. Contact the vet immediately for the necessary preparation, such as *Baycox*. Ensure that the birds have clean, dry litter. Warm, wet and fouled bedding provides the ideal conditions for the spread of the disease.

Digestive impaction

This, as the name suggests, is when there is a blockage in the upper area of the digestive system. It can be caused by eating twine or long coarse grass, or be gizzard worm infestation. The upper breast area feels hard to the touch.

Isolate the affected bird, without food but with plenty of clean water. One teaspoon of bicarbonate of soda in water followed by a teaspoon of medicinal liquid paraffin three or four times a day should clear it. Massage the area carefully to assist movement. If it does not clear up after a day or two, use a gizzard worming treatment. If this does not succeed, call in the vet who can operate to remove the obstruction. Ensure that there are no bits of baler twine, wire or other possible obstructive materials lying around where geese are grazing.

Cuts and wounds

Geese heal quickly from minor scratches, but an open wound needs to be treated immediately to prevent infection. Trim away feathers and loose skin making sure that bits do not come into contact with the wound. Wash thoroughly with clean warm water and apply antiseptic spray. Check regularly to make sure that there are no maggots and that infection has not set in. Toulouse geese, with their loose, open feathering are particularly vulnerable. If the wound is a large one, needing stitches, call the vet, as antibiotics may be needed. Prevention by protecting geese from dogs and foxes and dangerous materials like barbed wire is essential.

Diarrhoea

White diarrhoea flecked with blood, may be indicative of Coccidiosis in goslings, as referred to earlier. Greenish diarrhoea can be a sign of parasitic worm infestation (See Worms). Brownish diarrhoea that is also accompanied by slow growth and feathering may be an indication of Enteritis (See below).

Dropped tongue

This is caused when the bottom of the mouth drops between the lower jaws and the tongue falls into the gap. This is far more likely to occur with dewlap breeds like Toulouse or African. It can be permanently cured with a little operation. If you are not confident, a vet will do it. Make sure that the tongue is lifted and any material in the gap is removed, then stitch the loose skin below the jaw making sure that the inner membrane of the mouth is not included. Use close stitches. The loose skin sewn off will eventually wither and drop off (see diagram on page 91). Alternatively, a marble can be placed in the space and tied off above it until the skin shrivels and drops off, complete with marble. The cause is open to debate but leaving geese or goslings to feed on unsuitable fibrous material so that they eat frantically can cause the inside of the mouth to swell.

Egg problems

The most common egg problem is a blockage caused by an over-large egg stuck in the oviduct, although it is comparatively rare. If a goose is seen to be straining to no avail, coat the vent opening with a thin smear of *Vaseline* and squirt a little pure olive oil into the oviduct. Another method, after smearing the vent, is to hold the open vent over a steaming kettle, although you need to have a firm grip on the goose. If the steam temperature is alright for your hands it will not be too hot for the goose. The warm moist air encourages the oviduct to relax so that, hopefully, the egg emerges. If these methods do not work, call in the vet. Breaking the egg, pulling all the bits out and giving an antibiotic injection is a job for a professional.

Enteritis

This is caused by *E. coli* bacteria from dirty litter or other sources of contamination. Stress and sudden chilling of young birds can also reduce the ability of the body to fight it. There is likely to be brown diarrhoea, accompanied by slow growth and feathering. A vet should be consulted so that a treatment such as *Baytril* or *Terramycin* can be administered in the drinking water.

Eye problems

Sticky eye or *Ophthalmia* is a condition where there is a yellowish discharge that closes and sticks the eye. It can be aggravated by a diet deficient in essential vitamins, but the most frequent cause is a lack of clean water in which to immerse the head. Isolate the bird from the others and bathe the eye gently with a mild saline solution to clear the encrustations and administer antibiotic drops each evening until the condition has cleared up. Again, holding the goose firmly is essential, and the task is easier if two people are involved.

Provide a diet that is sufficiently high in protein and essential minerals and vitamins. A proprietary waterfowl laying or breeder's ration is suitable. Make sure that the isolated bird has a container of sterilised water so that it can fully immerse its head. Prevention is the best answer, however, so always give the appropriate balanced feed and clean water of sufficient depth.

Foot problems

Corns or callouses. These are on the bottom of the feet and can arise from wounds caused by walking over stony surfaces with sharp chippings, and not having fresh water to bathe the feet. Corns can be cauterized, cleaned with an antiseptic solution and dressed with an antibiotic cream. Keep the isolated bird on a deep bed of fresh straw and provide fresh sterilised water for bathing. Give it a proprietary balanced ration and some green feed. Wash and dress the wound daily until you are satisfied that it is no longer needed.

Bumble foot. This is a condition where the pad on the bottom of the foot swells up. Wash the foot with warm, soapy water, and remove the stone or splinter if it is still there, then apply antiseptic cream. If the original wound has healed over and there appears to be pus inside, apply a little *Vaseline* mixed with honey, which exerts an osmotic pressure, drawing the pus towards it. The isolation procedure is the same as for corns. Again, prevention is the best course of action. Do not allow geese to be driven or chased onto any sharp stony surface.

Leg problems

Leg weakness. This condition in goslings may arise from a dietary deficiency, particularly of niacin. Breeding stock should be given a purpose-made breeder ration, while a proprietary starter ration for goslings will also have the right balance of necessary minerals. If you cannot obtain these, and it is too cold for goslings to go outside, feed plenty of fresh, grass cuttings and brewer's yeast in water. This should correct the problem.

Straddled legs. This affects goslings and is where the legs slide outwards so that the bird does the splits. It is often caused by poor footing on a smooth surface. Ensure that their pen has a suitable surface so that their feet can walk without sliding about. A ribbed mat is suitable, or indeed anything that provides sufficient grip. Newly hatched goslings can be given a piece of old blanket until they have found their feet. Straddled or splayed legs can be treated by hobbling the gosling with wide, soft twine This enables it to walk but keeps the legs from splaying apart. (See page 68). If this does not work, you may have to put the bird down.

Staggers (Heat stress)

This is a condition that primarily afflicts geese, with symptoms of the bird staggering about and falling over. It is caused by over-heating that may arise from having insufficient drinking water and shade in hot conditions. It may also be the result of housing a goose in badly ventilated conditions. As referred to earlier, it is a bird of the outdoors and can cope with cold far better than heat.

Bring the affected bird into a cool place and encourage it to drink. Pouring a little cold water over the head can also be beneficial. If it is badly affected, plug in a fan to create a cool breeze.

Lice and mites

When geese are raised in proper conditions, external parasites are unlikely to be a problem. However, if you observe a goose scratching, then catch it and part the feathers of the area being scratched. Do so in good light as these parasites are very small. They can be dealt with by using a *Pyrethrum* based powder on the birds themselves, and then treating the housing or coop with *Barricade*.

If goslings are being raised by a broody hen, ensure that she is free of lice and mites beforehand. As always, prevention is best. Geese raised in clean surroundings, particularly those with access to swimming water are unlikely to be infested.

Vent gleet

Caused by the herpes virus, this venereal type disease is indicated by a nasty smelling discharge from the vent. There may also be encrustations around the vent. It may be possible to treat the bird (the vet will advise), but it may be necessary to put it down.

Wing problems

Slipped wing or Angel wing is a condition where a wing starts to hang down or project sideways, from about four weeks in the rapidly growing gosling. It is likely to be caused by having too much protein in the diet. Change the feed to wheat only immediately. Check the protein content of the feed for the rest of the flock and adjust it to around 14-15%.

Lift the slipped wing into the correct position and tape it into place. (See diagram opposite). After five days, remove the tape so that the wing can be exercised for a day. If the condition has not corrected itself, repeat the process. The important point is to act immediately as the longer the wing hangs down the harder it will be to correct it. There is some evidence that the condition is more prevalent in the fast growing heavy breeds. After six to seven weeks, the wing may fall a little again. This can also be corrected by taping it into the correct position for a short period. The procedure is effective in goslings but rarely so in adults.

Worms

There are a number of worms that can infest geese, but the two most troublesome are gapeworm and gizzard worm. Gapeworm gets into the throat and causes the bird to breathe harshly, cough and open and shut its beak in distress. Gizzard worm can also be very harmful. It burrows into the gizzard causing weakness, listlessness and loss of weight. (Suspect its presence if a young goose is sitting down a lot). In young birds, death can follow quickly so vigilance is needed.

All worms can be treated with *Flubenvet* mixed into the feed according to the manufacturer's instructions. This is the only wormer which is licensed for use with all poultry and waterfowl. All incoming geese should be wormed as a matter of course, and then twice a year after that. Prevent worm build up by always providing plenty of fresh water, preferably on a mesh stand to prevent a mucky area building up. Keep the birds on fresh ground as much as possible, and during periods of confined conditions, ensure that they have plenty of clean, deep, dry straw or wood shavings.

Dealing with dropped tongue

| The floor of the mouth has dropped and the tongue has fallen into it. | Clean out the space and sew where indicated by the dotted line, using close stitches. | The skin shrivels and eventually falls off. | Back to normal! |

If you are not confident to do this, a vet will do it for you. An alternative method is to place a marble in the space and then tie a thread above it, until the skin shrivels and falls off (along with the marble).

Slipped wing

The dotted line shows the normal position in which the wing is held against the body. The slipped wing may project downwards or even sideways.

There is not a great deal that can be done for an adult goose, but a gosling can have its wing taped to hold it in position. Photographic masking tape is effective because it peels off easily. Avoid feeding too much protein in the growing stage.

Reference section

Appendix I: **Regulations**

• Geese must be kept humanely and in accordance with their innate needs. They are protected by the *Welfare of Farmed Animals (England) Regulations 2000.*
• If geese are to be slaughtered, it must be according to the provisions of the *Welfare of Animals (Slaughter or Killing) Regulations 1995.* This requires that birds are stunned before being killed.
• Ornamental geese that are not native to Britain must be pinioned or kept in such a way that they cannot escape into the wild. They should have identifying leg rings.
• Geese that are being transported are protected by *The Welfare of Animals During Transport Order 1994.*
• Full details are available from the local *Animal Health Office (AHO)* of the *Trading Standards* office, and the local branch of the *Department of the Environment, Food and Rural Affairs (DEFRA).* DEFRA also has a Telephone Helpline: 08459 335577. Their website has a great deal of information, although it is not always easy to find your way around it: www.defra.gov.uk

Appendix II: **Daily and Seasonal Care**

Daily   • Check that run/enclosure/aviary door is secure then open house door.
  • Good morning geese!
  • Provide proprietary feed (if needed) in a clean, heavy-based feeder.
  • Observe birds for any signs of illness, limping, etc, while they are feeding.
  • Check drinkers and re-fill as necessary.
  • Collect any eggs.
  • Check nesting areas and litter, and replace litter as necessary.
  • Give grain feed in the afternoon (if necessary).
  • Check condition of pond or splashing water supply.
  • Ensure that all geese are inside. Good night geese!

Periodically
  • Clean out and refill pond, as necessary. Check other water courses.
  • Move moveable houses, as needed.
  • Check for signs of vermin such as rats, and take appropriate action.
  • Check pasture. Use new area as necessary. Lime old area and leave fallow to recover. If necessary, re-sow grass.
  • Clean out house or aviary.
  • Check fencing for security.
  • Check electric fencing current. Strim long grass that might 'short' current.
  • Mow or strim pasture to make new tillers of short grasses available.

Spring and summer
  • Ensure that nesting areas are available.
  • Prepare housing for broody hens, if used.
  • Check incubator if to be used.
  • Prepare brooding area.
  • Watch out for corvids stealing eggs.

- Buy goslings for rearing.
- Buy geese for future breeding.
- Observe performance of egg producers and keep production records.
- Watch out for signs of external and internal parasites.
- Worm new stock.

Autumn and winter
- Take action against predators and vermin.
- Buy (or sell) birds as future breeding stock.
- Worm breeding stock and give breeder's ration.
- Select birds for future show-winning potential. Send off for show schedules.
- Sell Michaelmas geese and then Christmas geese.
- Watch out for two-legged thieves!
- Harrow (rake) and lime pasture areas that are to be left fallow.
- Ensure that water supplies are not affected by frost.
- Prune trees in enclosures or aviary.

Further information
Books
Incubation: A Guide to Hatching and Rearing. K. Thear. Broad Leys Publishing Ltd.
Starting with Ducks. Katie Thear. Broad Leys Publishing Ltd.
The Smallholder's Manual. Katie Thear. The Crowood Press.
British Waterfowl Standards. C & M Ashton. British Waterfowl Association.
Domestic Geese. Chris Ashton. The Crowood Press.
Keeping Domestic Geese. Barbara Soames. Blandford Press.
Geese Breeding, Rearing and General Management. R. Appleyard. Poultry World.
The Book of Geese. Dave Holderread. Hen House Publications.
Ornamental Waterfowl. Johnson and Payn. Saiga Publishing.
Manual of Ornamental Waterfowl. Simon Tarsnane. British Waterfowl Association.
Wildfowl at Home. Alan Birkbeck. Gold Cockerel Series.

Organisations
The British Waterfowl Association. Tel: 01892 740212. www.waterfowl.org
Domestic Waterfowl Club. Tel: 01488 638014 (evenings). www.domestic-waterfowl.co.uk
The Goose Club. Tel: 01437 563308. www.gooseclub.org.uk
Poultry Club of Great Britain. Tel: 01205 724081. www.poultryclub.org
The British Goose Producers' Association. Tel: 020 7202 4760. www.goose.cc
American Livestock Breeds Conservancy. www.albc-usa.org
Aviornis UK. Tel: 01625 573287. www.aviornis.co.uk
The Wildfowl and Wetlands Trust. Tel: 01453 891900. www.wwt.org.uk
The Humane Slaughter Association. Tel: 01582 831919. www.hsa.org.uk

Collections
Blackbrook Zoological Park. BWA conservation and education centre. (Staffs).
Tel: 01538 308293.
The Domestic Fowl Trust. (Worcs). Tel: 01386 833083. www.domesticfowltrust.co.uk
Slimbridge Wildfowl & Wetlands Trust (Glos) Tel: 01453 891900. www.wwt.org.uk
Kintaline Poultry & Waterfowl Farm (Argyll). Tel: 01631 720223. www.kintaline.co.uk

Suppliers

Pure-bred stock Make sure that they come from a reputable stockist. The *BWA* has a Breeders' Directory. *Country Smallholding* magazine also has a Breeders' Directory in every issue. This is also listed on their website at www.countrysmallholding.com

Commercial stock
Lancashire Geese. Tel: 01695 572023.
Norfolk Geese. Tel: 01379 676391.
Wessex Geese. Tel: 01963 251114

Housing
The Domestic Fowl Trust. Tel: 01386 833083. www.domesticfowltrust.co.uk
Forsham Cottage Arks. Tel: 0800 163797. www.forshamcottagearks.com
Gardencraft. Tel: 01766 513036. www.gcraft.co.uk
Smiths Sectional Buildings. Tel: 0115 9254722

Incubators Not all small incubators are suitable for goose eggs. Check before buying.
Aliwal Incubators. Tel: 01508 489328
Brinsea Products Ltd. Tel: 01934 823039. www.brinsea.co.uk
Interhatch. Tel: 0114 2552340
M S Incubators. Tel: 0116 247 8335.
Solway Feeders Ltd (also pluckers). Tel: 01557 500253. www.solwayfeeders.com
Southern Aviaries. Tel: 01825 830930.
Traditional Poultry & Game Supplies. Tel: 01603 738292.

Goose Feeds
Allen and Page. Tel: 01362 822900. www.smallholderfeed.co.uk
BOCM Pauls Ltd. Tel: 01757 244000. www.bocmpauls.co.uk
Clark and Butcher Ltd. Tel: 01353 720237.
Mazuri Zoo Foods. Tel: 01376 511260. www.mazuri.com
Slimbridge Wildfowl Feeds. Tel: 01285 658884
W. H. Marriage and Sons Ltd. Tel: 01245 612000 www.marriagefeeds.co.uk

Electric Fencing
Apel Ltd. Tel: 01790 754810. www.electricfencingdirect.co.uk
Electranets Ltd. Tel: 01452 617841
Electric Fencing Solutions. Tel: 01732 833976. www.electricfencing.co.uk
Hotline Renco Ltd. Tel: 01626 331188. www.hotline-fencing.co.uk
G.A. and M.J. Strange. Tel: 01225 891236.

Pest Control
Acorn Pest Control. Tel: 02476 491689. www.acorn-pest-control.co.uk
Amtex. Tel: 01568 610900. www.thezapper.co.uk
Breckland International. Tel: 01760 756414.
Sorex Ltd. Tel: 0151 420 7151.

General equipment
Ascott Smallholding Supplies. Tel: 0845 130 6285. www.ascott-shop.com
Domestic Fowl Trust. Tel: 01386 833083. www.domesticfowltrust.co.uk
Oxmoor Smallholder Supplies. Tel: 01757 288186.
Parkland Products. www.parklandproducts.co.uk
Pintail Sporting Services. Tel: 01794 524472.
Sedgbeer Processing Supplies. (pluckers) Tel: 01373 836589.
Stock Nutrition. (pluckers). Tel: 01362 851200.

Index

Broad Leys Publishing Limited

Specialising in poultry, waterfowl and smallholding books.
Our other titles include the following:

Starting with Chickens Katie Thear	£6.95
Starting with Bantams David Scrivener	£7.95
Starting with Ducks Katie Thear	£7.95
Incubation Katie Thear.	£6.95
Organic Poultry Katie Thear	£12.95
Keeping Quail Katie Thear	£7.95
Starting with a Smallholding David Hills.	£7.95
Starting with Sheep Mary Castell	£7.95
Starting with Pigs Andy Case	£7.95
Starting with Bees Peter Gordon	£7.95
Cheesemaking and Dairying Katie Thear	£7.95
Build Your Own Poultry House & Run	£3.00

Also available are

Free-Range Poultry Katie Thear	£17.50
The Smallholder's Manual Katie Thear	£23.00

Titles may be ordered from bookshops or purchased direct from the publisher.
They are post-free from the address below or from our secure on-line bookshop.

Broad Leys Publishing Ltd
1 Tenterfields, Newport, Saffron Walden, Essex CB11 3UW, UK.
Tel/Fax: 01799 541065 (International calls - (+) 1799 541065)
E-mail: kdthear@btinternet.com
Website: www.blpbooks.co.uk